Date Due

Organizational Surveys

Management Applications Series

Alan C. Filley, University of Wisconsin, Madison
Series Editor

Performance in Organizations: Determinants and Appraisal
L. L. Cummings, University of Wisconsin, Madison
Donald P. Schwab, University of Wisconsin, Madison

Leadership and Effective Management
Fred E. Fiedler, University of Washington
Martin M. Chemers, University of Utah

Managing by Objectives
Anthony P. Raia, University of California, Los Angeles

Organizational Change: Techniques and Applications
Newton Margulies, University of California, Irvine
John C. Wallace, University of California, Irvine

Interpersonal Conflict Resolution
Alan C. Filley, University of Wisconsin, Madison

*Group Techniques for Program Planning: A Guide to Nominal
Group and Delphi Processes*
Andre L. Delbecq, University of Wisconsin, Madison
Andrew H. Van de Ven, University of Pennsylvania
David H. Gustafson, University of Wisconsin, Madison

Organizational Behavior Modification
Fred Luthans, University of Nebraska, Lincoln
Robert Kreitner, Arizona State University

Task Design and Employee Motivation
Ramon J. Aldag, University of Wisconsin, Madison
Arthur P. Brief, University of Iowa

*Organizational Surveys: An Internal Assessment of Organizational
Health*
Randall B. Dunham, University of Wisconsin, Madison
Frank J. Smith, Sears, Roebuck and Company

Organizational Surveys

An Internal Assessment of Organizational Health

Randall B. Dunham

University of Wisconsin, Madison

Frank J. Smith

Sears, Roebuck and Company

Scott, Foresman and Company   Glenview, Illinois
Dallas, Tex.   Oakland, N.J.   Palo Alto, Cal.
Tucker, Ga.   London, England

Dedicated to Susanne Rowe Dunham
and
In Memory of Hellena "Monie" Bowers

Grateful acknowledgment is made for permission to reprint or adapt the following:

Table 2.1: from Herzberg, F., Mausner, B. *The Motivation to Work*. Copyright 1959 by John Wiley and Sons, Inc. Reprinted by permission.   Figure 2.2: from Porter, Lyman W., Lawler, Edward E., III, *MANAGERIAL ATTITUDES AND PERFORMANCE* (Homewood, Ill.: Richard D. Irwin, 1968) p. 429. © 1968 by Richard D. Irwin, Inc. Used with permission.   Table 3.2: from Porter, L., Steers, R. "Organization, Work and Personal Factors in Employee Turnovers and Absenteeism," *Psychological Bulletin*. Copyright 1973 by The American Psychological Association. Reprinted by permission.   Figure 3.2: reprinted by permission from *MOTIVATION AND COMMITMENT*, Vol. II of the ASPA Handbook of Personnel and Industrial Relations, D. Yoder and H. G. Heneman, Jr., eds., copyright © 1975 by The Bureau of National Affairs, Inc., Washington, D. C. 20037.   Figure 3.2: from March, J., Simon, H. *Organizations*. Copyright 1958 by John Wiley and Sons, Inc. Reprinted by permission.   Table 3.3: from Hulin, Charles. "Satisfaction and Turnover in a Female Clerical Population," *Journal of Applied Psychology*. Copyright 1966 by The American Psychological Association. Reprinted by permission.   Table 3.4: from Smith, Frank J. "Work Attitudes as Predictors of Attendance on a Specific Day," *Journal of Applied Psychology*. Copyright 1977 by The American Psychological Association. Reprinted by permission.   Table 3.5: from Vroom, Victor. *Work and Motivation*. Copyright 1964 by John Wiley and Sons, Inc. Reprinted by permission.   Table 4.1: from Krejcie, R., Morgan, D. "Determining Sample Size for Research Activities," *Educational and Psychological Measurement*. Copyright 1970 by *Educational and Psychological Measurement*. Reprinted by permission.   Table 4.2: from Hulin, C. L.; Kendall, L. M.; Smith, P. C. *The Measurement of Satisfaction in Work and Retirement: A Strategy for the Study of Attitudes*. Copyright 1975 by Bowling Green State University. Reprinted by permission.   Table 4.3: from Dawis, Rene; England, George; Lofquist, Lloyd; Weiss, David. *Manual for the Minnesota Satisfaction Questionnaire*. Copyright 1967 by the University of Minnesota. Reprinted by permission.   Table 4.4: from Smith, Frank J. "Index of Organizational Reactions," *Catalog of Selected Documents in Psychology*. Copyright 1976 by the American Psychological Association. Reprinted by permission.   Table 4.5: from Kunin, Theodore. "The Construction of a New Type of Attitude Measure," *Personnel Psychology*. Copyright 1955. Reprinted by permission of General Motors Corporation, *Personnel Psychology*, and the author.   Table 4.5: from Dunham, R. B., Herman, J. B. "Development of a Female Faces Scale for Measuring Job Satisfaction," *Journal of Applied Psychology*. Copyright 1975 by The American Psychological Association. Reprinted by permission.   Figure 5.1: from THE CORE SURVEY. Copyright 1962, Science Research Associates, Inc. Reprinted by permission of the publisher.   Figures 5.2–5.12: reprinted by permission of Frank J. Smith.   Appendix III: adapted from "Validation of the Index of Organizational Reactions with the JDI, the MSQ, and the Faces Scales," by Randall Dunham, Frank J. Smith, and Richard S. Blackburn. ACADEMY OF MANAGEMENT JOURNAL 1977, Vol. 20, No. 3, 420–432. Reprinted by permission.

Library of Congress Cataloging in Publication Data

Dunham, Randall B

   Organizational surveys.

   Includes bibliographies and index.

   1. Employee attitude surveys.   I. Smith, Frank J., 1927–   joint author.   II. Title.

HF5549.5.A83D86   658.3   78-25544

ISBN 0-673-15143-3

1 2 3 4 5 6 7-EBI-84 83 82 81 80 79 78

Series Foreword

The Management Applications Series is concerned with the application of contemporary research, theory, and techniques. There are many excellent books at advanced levels of knowledge, but there are few which address themselves to the application of such knowledge. The authors in this series are uniquely qualified for this purpose, since they are all scholars who have experience in implementing change in real organizations through the methods they write about.

Each book treats a single topic in depth. Where the choice is between presenting many approaches briefly or a single approach thoroughly, we have opted for the latter. Thus, after reading the book, the student or practitioner should know how to apply the methodology described.

Selection of topics for the series was guided by contemporary relevance to management practice, and by the availability of an author qualified as an expert, yet able to write at a basic level of understanding. No attempt is made to cover all management methods, nor is any sequence implied in the series, although the books do complement one another. For example, change methods might fit well with managing by objectives.

The books in this series may be used in several ways. They may be used to supplement textbooks in basic courses on management, organizational behavior, personnel, or industrial psychology/sociology. Students appreciate the fact that the material is immediately applicable. Practicing managers will want to use individual books to increase their skills, either through self-study or in connection with management development programs, inside or outside the organization.

Alan C. Filley

Foreword

It may be somewhat unusual for a businessman to introduce a book in a behavioral science series. In the case of the survey process, however, it seems very much in order, for perhaps in no other area does the business person possess a greater responsibility for the successful application of a behavioral technique. In fact, it has been my experience in widely different business settings that while survey results provide management with a sound decision-making base, their appropriate utilization (and the organizational growth that can result from it) occurs only to the extent that management is willing to accept the findings and to act on them. It is also my conviction, again born of experience, that management is well advised to listen and to respond to employees. In almost every organization, employees have something to tell management which it should, but does not, know.

In some cases, this employee-generated information can encourage direct action by underscoring management's resolve, while in others it may suggest the reconsideration of a management position or contemplated action. Examples of each come to mind. The first example involved a communications station. A decision to install sophisticated automated equipment had been seriously reconsidered by local management because of increasing concern that technicians would resent and resist such a move. It was found that this concern stemmed from the comments of several highly vocal members of the technical crew. A later survey of this group, however, clearly indicated that far from being resentful of or intimidated by the new equipment, the majority of the technicians welcomed it and saw it as an opportunity and a challenge to develop and use new skills. With this information, management was able to proceed with a change that greatly benefited the station and improved the overall satisfaction of the employees.

The other example involved a ski resort where survey results may have helped to avert a possible disaster. These results, obtained as part of a routine survey of the ski lift operators, indicated a very strong feeling that equipment on one lift was rapidly deteriorating. Since this was directly contrary to insurance and safety inspection reports that had been obtained earlier, local management at first dismissed this disquieting finding. It soon reconsidered, however, and conducted a special test of all lifts, only to find that a number of chairs on one lift were in danger of falling. Because the survey brought this information to the attention of management and encouraged it to focus on an immediate problem, it is very possible that injury and even loss of life was avoided, to say nothing of the considerable financial liability the company might have incurred.

Going beyond these specific cases, I think one could argue that all important management or business decisions by definition occur in the face of conflicting facts and ambiguity, and any technique that serves to lessen this uncertainty should be seriously considered. It is because I as a businessman believe that the survey process does reduce uncertainty that I am happy to introduce this book.

Edgar B. Stern, Jr.
Member of the Board of Directors
Sears, Roebuck and Co.

Preface

Surveys can provide a tremendous variety of benefits for organizations. They can be used to assess employee attitudes about organizational policies, to diagnose existing or potential problems, to enhance communication between different levels of an organization, and for many other purposes. These benefits, however, are likely to be realized only if the survey process is thoroughly understood and appropriately administered. Unfortunately, very little information on the subject has been available; too often, survey efforts by misinformed managers have produced dysfunctional results. The goal of this book, then, is to provide practicing managers and those aspiring to be managers with the expertise necessary to conduct surveys properly and to use the results effectively.

The book outlines procedures for developing, administering, and interpreting organizational surveys. Standard survey questionnaires are presented and evaluated. The development of special survey questionnaires designed for specific situations is also discussed. In addition, we explore the theoretical basis for surveys because we are convinced that an understanding of theory enhances the manager's ability to administer and evaluate surveys. The primary focus of the book, however, is on the practical application of survey techniques. Throughout the book, we use actual examples of successful surveys to supplement our discussion of these techniques.

We have drawn from a wide variety of experiences with organizational surveys in writing this book. One of us has designed and conducted surveys for one of the oldest continuous organizational programs in the United States. And one of us has served as a survey consultant for many different kinds of organizations. In addition, we have relied on our own research on survey development and validation as well as on the significant research that has been published on job satisfaction. We believe the book represents a thorough treatment of the topic.

   We wish to express our appreciation to Charles Bacon for making available much of the information used in this book; to Jon Bentz, for his contributions to the development of systematic survey programs; to Tom Comeaux, for his contributions to every chapter of the book; to Cathy Bell and Dick Blackburn, for their careful reading of the manuscript and their suggestions, which led to a number of improvements in the book; and to Charles Schaff at Scott, Foresman, for his editorial assistance. We are also indebted to Janice Kolbaska and Chris Kozak, who patiently prepared the manuscript; to Dr. Beth Smith, who provided helpful suggestions and encouragement; and to Paula, Geoffrey, Wanda, Larry, and Grant, who missed a number of weekends because of this book. Finally, we wish to thank the Dunhams—Bob, Marie, Terry, Christie, and Cindy—for their support and interest; and Susanne, for her encouragement, tolerance, and understanding.

R. B. D.
F. J. S.

Contents

Organizational Surveys: 1
An Overview

Historically, interest in organizational surveys was based primarily on the belief that "the happy worker is the productive worker." The logical argument that frustration on the job would lead to poor job performance while satisfaction on the job would lead to good job performance proved appealing to theorists *and* practitioners. In fact, assumptions of this sort predominated during the 1930s and 1940s and provided the basis for the development of a number of extensive organizational survey programs. The results of a series of research studies conducted in the 1950s and 1960s, however, failed to support this simple relationship of job satisfaction to performance. Still, this research (examined later in this book) did demonstrate a fairly consistent link between job satisfaction and withdrawal behaviors such as absenteeism and turnover.

Until the 1960s, organizational surveys were legitimized primarily through reference to the relationship of job satisfaction to behavior. During the 1960s, job satisfaction began to be widely recognized as an important topic in its own right. It became a legitimate social issue rivaling the problem of unemployment. Job dissatisfaction was believed to trouble a majority of the work force, but unemployment affected only a minority of the work force. Special task forces were created to investigate phenomena known as "blue-collar blues" and "white-collar woes." Job satisfaction (or at least dissatisfaction) had come of age as an issue to be dealt with as an end in itself, and a new interest in organizational surveys emerged.

In the last decade two developments expanded interest in organizational surveys once again. First, new research on the relationship of satisfaction to performance suggested that under certain conditions the happy worker may, indeed, be the productive worker. Second, economic criteria were used to demonstrate the fiscal importance of job satisfaction to profit-making organizations. The possible realization of substantial monetary dividends renewed interest in organizational surveys and refocused attention on organizational effectiveness.

The level of worker job satisfaction, which has such an important impact on profits and organizational effectiveness, reflects the state of organizational health. Just as the term *health* refers to more than just good health, the term *satisfaction* (as used in this book) refers to more than just satisfied workers. Measures of satisfaction obtained from surveys can range from very positive to very negative.

PURPOSE OF THE BOOK

As we move into the 1980s, many organizations, large and small, are conducting organizational surveys, and many more are seriously considering the technique. Unfortunately, there is very little guidance available for organizations contemplating the use of surveys. Providing this guidance is the main purpose of this book.

In the absence of such guidance, organizations have taken several approaches. First, they have designed in-house surveys with little direction from the professional discipline. This approach has occasionally succeeded well and occasionally failed completely. More often, it has produced survey programs which fall short of their potential. Second, they have employed internal or external consultants to aid in the design and implementation of survey programs. This approach has worked well in most cases but, of course, has the advantages and drawbacks experienced whenever organizations contract for any professional service.

Moreover, it is difficult to choose and evaluate a consultant's service when members of the organization have little understanding of the techniques involved.

Third, organizations have patterned their programs after those used by other organizations. This approach can be helpful, but there are several potential drawbacks. If the model company has a poor program, the result is likely to be another deficient program. Even if the model company or organization has a successful program, there is no guarantee that it will be the best for another organization. In general, the more similar the two organizations and their employees, the better the chances are that the system that worked for one company will work for another. But an organization with a successful survey program may be reluctant to share it with others because it usually knows that the program contributes to organizational effectiveness and sharpens its competitive edge. Such an organization will probably view its survey program with an intense proprietary interest.

A second purpose of this book is to examine and reduce some of the abuses of organizational surveys. Though most of these stem from ignorance rather than from bad intent, the results have been at best, less than optimal and at worst, dysfunctional. This book, therefore, discusses the knowledge needed to plan, implement, and evaluate an organizational survey program. It should be useful for the training of in-house survey teams and for the education of managerial personnel who must deal with internal or external survey consultants and who must ultimately respond to survey results.

ISSUES TO BE COVERED

This book covers the major issues that need to be considered by any organization currently utilizing surveys or contemplating their use. It focuses on satisfaction with work and the work environment—the state of organizational health—and discusses the various sources of satisfaction. Chapter Two provides an overview of the relevant theories and research. Chapter Three examines the major reasons for conducting surveys. It considers the role of the survey as a feedback device, as a diagnostic tool, as a training technique, and as a means for improving communication and job-related attitudes.

Because the book is designed for managers, the ultimate

consumers of organizational surveys, it focuses primarily on the application of survey techniques. Chapters Four and Five present specific techniques for developing, conducting, administering, and interpreting organizational surveys. Actual survey applications supplement the presentation of these techniques. Chapters Four and Five also explore the spectrum of choices facing the manager who conducts an organizational survey. These choices range from the selection of survey questions to the selection of employee sample to the interpretation of survey results. For some of these choices, we make specific recommendations and offer support for our preferences. For others, we discuss alternative approaches and examine the factors that must be considered in order to make an intelligent decision.

CRITICAL TERMS AND CONCEPTS

Some definitions of critical terms used throughout the book may be helpful at this point. These terms, widely used and abused, include *survey, attitude, job satisfaction,* and *opinion.* Because most of these terms are ambiguous, it is important to specify the meanings we attach to them.

A *survey,* according to *Webster's New World Dictionary,* involves a careful examination for some specific purpose. Organizational surveys, as discussed in this book, refer to careful, detailed examinations of the perceptions, attitudes, and opinions of members of organizations. The general purpose of the survey is to obtain a better understanding of employee reactions and preferences. Such knowledge should help optimize organizational effectiveness and employee satisfaction. Survey results can be used to achieve the following: 1) reduction of turnover, absenteeism, and tardiness; 2) increases in employees' efforts toward organizational effectiveness; 3) analysis of known problems; 4) identification of potential problems; and 5) evaluation of current policies and practices.

The organizational survey primarily uses pencil-and-paper questionnaires or structured interviews to obtain desired information. The survey process includes reports to management and to workers on the findings of the survey. This feedback generally will *not* include information about an individual worker's responses but instead will focus on the responses of meaningful groups of workers, e.g., a group of persons with similar jobs, tenure levels, ages, training, etc. Only in rare cases—usually for specific research purposes—are individuals asked to provide personal identification.

The word *attitude* describes a person's complex set of beliefs, feelings, and behavioral tendencies about another person or thing. Every attitude has cognitive, affective, and behavioral components. It is important to distinguish between these three to understand fully the formation, change, and importance of attitudes.

The *cognitive component* of an attitude summarizes and organizes the individual's information about the object of the attitude. This component constitutes the individual's set of *beliefs* about the object. It is important to note that this set of beliefs is based on what the person thinks is true and does not necessarily represent completely accurate information. The cognitive element of an attitude is heavily influenced by the individual's perceptual process. Thus, errors in perception often lead either to the selective omission of information or to the inclusion of inaccurate information about the object.

In its purest form, the cognitive component consists only of the individual's set of information about the object. It does not include the person's feelings or behavioral intentions toward the object. For example, the cognitive component of a worker's attitude toward a co-worker, Susanne Brown, could include the information that she is a thirty-four-year-old woman with a Harvard M.B.A. who has been with the company for only five years, but has been promoted seven times and is being paid a salary of $38,000 as a manager of a department with a budget of a million dollars per year. The cognitive component could also include the beliefs that she has been promoted primarily because she is a woman and that she is willing to take advantage of her co-workers in order to further her own career. These pieces of information are part of the person's attitude toward Susanne Brown even though they may not all be accurate. It may well be true that Susanne Brown is a female with a Harvard M.B.A. who controls a department with a million-dollar-a-year budget. It may also be true that she has often taken advantage of other workers to promote her own best interests. In actuality, however, she may be a person who is thirty-nine years old, her promotions may have been based on excellent performance, and she may be currently making $31,000 per year. The cognitive component of other workers' attitudes toward this female manager may vary widely. Each of these people may in fact possess unique attitudes toward this woman.

The *affective component* of an attitude consists of the person's *feelings* toward an object. This component involves human emotion and is expressed as like or dislike for the object. It is heavily dependent upon the cognitive component of the attitude, since the affective component is essentially an indication of the way the person reacts to the cognitive element of the attitude.

Evaluative processes influence feelings just as perceptual processes influence cognitions. The fact that two people have very similar beliefs about an object does not necessarily mean that they will share similar feelings toward that object. For example, two people may believe that the manager, Susanne Brown, is earning $38,000 per year but have very different feelings about this piece of information. One person may feel positively about this piece of information because he or she believes that it identifies a competent co-worker. Another person may react negatively to this piece of information because he or she is making considerably less than $38,000.

Affective components of attitudes are complex. Although people tend to organize their feelings into a relatively consistent framework, they are capable of reacting differently to various components of an object or person. Thus, a person might have favorable feelings toward a superior as a competent manager but unfavorable feelings toward the superior as a friend. It is likely that both the cognitive and affective components of other people's attitudes toward this manager will vary.

The final element of an attitude, the *behavioral component,* summarizes the *tendencies for the person's behavior* toward the attitude object. Both the cognitive and affective components influence the behavioral component. For example, if you believe that a person has problem-solving information that you do not possess, you are more likely to go to that person for assistance than if you believe that he or she knows less than you do. Similarly, you are more likely to interact socially with someone you like than with someone you dislike.

The fact that two people share many similar beliefs and feelings toward a person does not necessarily mean that they will behave toward that person in the same manner. Two people might agree that the manager of their department often takes advantage of subordinates but is a competent accountant. Both may dislike the manager. However, their behavioral intentions toward that person may be very different. The first person may avoid the manager as much as possible in order to avoid displeasure. The second person, however, may intend to interact with the manager a great deal in order to maximize the chances of being promoted. As with the other components of an attitude, the behavioral component is complex and often varies from person to person.

In summary, attitudes consist of three separate components. These components correspond to the following three questions:

1) How would you describe the object? (Cognitive—"This company is large.")
2) How do you feel about the object? (Affective—"I dislike this company.")
3) How do you intend to act toward the object? (Behavioral—"I am going to leave this company.")

Attitudes may be learned in three ways. The most direct way of acquiring an attitude is through actual experience with the object. For example, a person's attitude toward a manager may be based on actual interaction with that manager. It may be acquired through association with some other object for which an attitude has already been formed. For example, workers' attitudes toward previous managers may influence their attitudes toward a new manager. If an employee has repeatedly experienced competent managers, it is likely that a new manager will also be expected to be competent. Finally, attitudes may be acquired through a social learning process. When a new worker joins a work team, peers usually provide information about the supervisor. This interchange influences the worker's attitude toward the supervisor even in the absence of personal interaction.

Although attitudes are typically most influenced by personal experience, social influences can also be very powerful. In fact, most attitudes in organizations are influenced by all three sources. *The implication of this is that action plans designed to change attitudes will meet with some degree of resistance if they influence only one of these sources of attitudes.*

There is some confusion surrounding the specific meaning of the term *job satisfaction*. There is general agreement that the concept involves workers' attitudes toward their work and work environment. But does job satisfaction encompass all three components of an attitude? Is job satisfaction a general reaction to the total work environment? Do people have specific levels of satisfaction for different elements of the work environment? This book will address satisfaction primarily as it relates to the affective component of attitudes. Job satisfaction includes the set of affective reactions (feelings) of employees to the work and work environment.

As already pointed out, the affective component of attitudes is usually complex. Accordingly, job satisfaction consists of a set of specific satisfactions called *facets* of satisfaction. These are measured as reactions to separate dimensions of the work and work environment, i.e., satisfaction with pay, supervision, etc. Although each of these dimensions of the environment has its major impact on the corresponding facet of satisfaction, there is typically a moderate spillover onto other facets. For example, satisfaction with promotional opportunities may also have some effect on satisfaction with pay. The term *general job satisfaction* is used to describe the individual's overall affective reaction to the set of work and work environment factors; it is a function of all of the facets of satisfaction. Note, however, that two individuals with similar levels of overall job satisfaction may not react the same way to each facet of satisfaction.

This definition of general job satisfaction clearly implies a "compensatory" model in which high satisfaction on one facet can compensate for relatively low satisfaction on another facet. Such a model should not, however, lead to the conclusion that we need not be concerned about a low level of satisfaction for a particular facet as long as it is balanced by relatively high satisfaction on other facets. There are two problems with such an approach. First, different satisfaction facets are likely to correspond to different behavioral intentions for workers. For example, dissatisfaction with pay may cause a worker to seek another job, whereas dissatisfaction with co-workers might cause a worker to try to avoid them. Second, the importance of particular facets varies for different individuals and situations. Consider the case of a worker who has had a series of illnesses and who has only two years until retirement. This worker, unlike a healthy, twenty-

one-year-old college graduate, will probably attach little importance to promotional opportunities but considerable importance
to medical and pension plans.

Research on job satisfaction has identified a number of
satisfaction facets that are important to most individuals:

1) Company policies and practices
2) Compensation
3) Co-worker relations
4) Physical conditions of the environment
5) Promotional opportunities
6) Supervision skills and relations
7) Work: Amount and demands
8) Work: Characteristics of the work itself.

Other facets of work and the work environment can be important,
depending upon the workers and the situation. These include
factors such as ability utilization, achievement, social service, and
social status.

Because job satisfaction consists of human feelings, it is
impossible to measure directly. We are forced to infer satisfaction
levels from things that people say or do. Fortunately, several
comprehensive research efforts have led to the development of
good measures of job satisfaction. These instruments of measurement are discussed in Chapter Four of this book.

The term *opinion* has also been used with a variety of
meanings in the context of organizational surveys. Various people
have used this term exactly as we have used the terms *attitude,
belief,* or *satisfaction.* In fact, the first two definitions of *opinion* in
Webster's New World Dictionary correspond to our definitions of
the cognitive component (beliefs) and the affective component
(feelings) of attitudes. *Webster's* third definition, however, allows
us to distinguish *opinions* as a separate type of information that
can be tapped by organizational surveys. An *opinion* is "the formal judgment of an expert on a matter in which his advice is
sought" (*Webster's New World Dictionary,* 1966, p. 1028). Note
that the term *expert* in the definition of *opinion* is appropriate. In
general, workers at all levels of an organization possess some form
of expertise that can be of real value to the organization when
reflected in an opinion survey.

Surveys are frequently used to obtain workers' opinions

on organizational issues. For example, the management at Sears, Roebuck, and Company recently considered instituting a four-day, forty-hour (4-40) work schedule for a group of workers. They surveyed workers and department managers to determine their preferences for the 4-40 schedule and to solicit their opinions on the effect of a 4-40 schedule on work coverage. The result was that management adopted a 4-40 work week, which has benefited workers as well as the organization.

Although this book focuses primarily on worker satisfaction, it also considers worker opinions and all three components of attitudes. This approach is necessary in order to understand more fully the sources and implications of employee job satisfaction and to maximize the utility of each worker in increasing organizational effectiveness.

METHODS OF OBTAINING SURVEY DATA

Several methods can be used to obtain survey information. The most common of these are observation, interview, and questionnaire. There are advantages and disadvantages associated with each technique.

Most organizations use the observation method to obtain survey information. In many organizations, this is the only type of data gathered. Most managers believe that they acquire a considerable amount of knowledge about worker attitudes and opinions through formal and informal interactions with their employees. Undeniably, this sort of unstructured observational technique does provide a good deal of valid information. Unfortunately, it can also provide a good deal of distorted information. The personal observations of a manager are greatly limited by his or her interpersonal sensitivity and by possible preoccupation with other responsibilities. In addition, the workers' dependence upon their managers for continued employment and income can inhibit or disguise their real feelings.

It is sometimes difficult for managers to realize that this dependence can distort their perceptions about workers' attitudes. Indeed, this is one of the major insights achieved by managers who have participated as interviewers on survey teams in many organizations. Because this program trains managers to listen to employees and only allows managers to participate in surveys of units other than their own (where workers do not feel dependent on them), they are often amazed by employees' reactions to supervisors. Invariably, managers realize that their own employees would probably give the same kind of information. As a result, managers become acutely aware of the subtle nature of the leader-subordinate relationship.

Observational techniques are further limited because they are usually insensitive to future events or intentions. Often workers' dissatisfaction does not become evident until after the occurrence of dysfunctional events. To use a medical analogy, the observation technique is best suited to a postmortem examination rather than to an early diagnosis that can allow treatment. In fact, one of the serious problems in many organizations is that management becomes concerned with employee attitudes only after they have had a negative impact on organizational effectiveness.

Some of the limitations of personal observation can be reduced through the use of structured observation techniques. These techniques provide rules for the systematic observation and recording of behavioral data. They can help to define the scope and increase the accuracy of the data.

Interviews can also play an important role in the organizational survey process. A well-conducted interview can obtain information that is not readily available through the observation process. Although attitudes and opinions cannot be directly observed, a skilled interviewer can elicit this type of psychological data from the worker. The interview process is considerably more efficient than observational techniques. For example, critical incidents covering a long segment of time can be discussed during the course of a relatively short interview. The interview can also be used to project into the future, exploring the subject's behavioral intentions and reactions to anticipated events. Observation can provide a description of an event, but an in-depth interview can produce an explanation or interpretation of the event.

Consider the following example. The Hanover Radio Company employs 375 workers to assemble portable transistor radios. The company had been suffering high costs due to returns and warranty repair work. In an attempt to decrease the number of defective radios being manufactured, the president of the company sent a letter to all workers, informing them that the work of Hanover Radio Company employees was well below the industry standard and that such poor performance would no longer be tolerated. According to the letter, if the work did not improve, 10 percent of the workers would be laid off. Soon after this letter was sent to employees, the average work-team productivity level dropped from 50 radios per hour to 40. The president of the company responded to this drop in productivity by sending another letter to all employees. In this letter he informed the employees that he would not tolerate a work slowdown in protest to his pressure for improving work quality. He imposed an immediate wage reduction of 10 percent on the workers until productivity returned to its former level. In the two weeks following the president's second letter, productivity dropped even further, 42 workers quit their jobs, and 75 percent of the remaining employees signed election-authorization cards in an attempt to introduce a union to the company.

In the case of the Hanover Radio Company, observational techniques yielded accurate information about low-quality radios and decreases in productivity. A series of interviews conducted with employees three weeks after the president's second letter, however, revealed that the president had incorrectly interpreted this information. The following is a composite of workers' comments from several of these interviews:

> When I received the first letter from the president, I was surprised and hurt. I had never been told that there was any serious quality problem with our radios and I had always been proud of my work. Anyhow, during lunch breaks that next week most of us talked a lot about how we could improve our quality. We decided that the best thing to do would be to slow down a little and make sure each and every radio was put together exactly right. We agreed that we would show our president that we could do things right. After all, Hanover Radio had always taken pretty good care of us and this was the first time the president had really acted like a son-of-a-bitch.

> When that second letter came things changed right away. Here we were breaking our backs trying to help the company and that old guy rewards us by cutting our pay. Some of the guys got so mad that they took a couple of sick

days and went job hunting—quite a few of them even took other jobs. The rest of us decided that, if we were going to be paid less, we would work less. We also decided that it was time to listen to the people who had been talking about forming a union so that this kind of thing couldn't happen again.

It is obvious that interviews could have been very helpful to the Hanover Radio Company if conducted earlier.

Hiring and/or training interviewers can be quite expensive and may not always be justified. On the other hand, the training may have beneficial effects that go well beyond the limited purpose of conducting a survey. When management personnel are used as interviewers, the cost may be regarded as a sound investment in managerial development.

Interviews involve face-to-face contact between employees and interviewers. Unless they are well trained, the interviewers may induce error in a number of ways:

1) The interviewer's facial expressions, manner, or personal characteristics can bias the interviewee's answers;
2) The interviewer's frame of reference can influence the manner in which comments are interpreted;
3) The working of questions can have a major impact on the data obtained;
4) The use of strongly polarized alternatives can make it difficult for a respondent to frame an answer; and
5) Leading questions can bias the interviewee's response.

Appendix I presents a guide for nondirective interviewing. It emphasizes the use of interviews as complements to the questionnaire method. Most of the issues addressed in Appendix I, however, would also be valid for more generalized interview approaches.

The pencil-and-paper questionnaire is the most common method for obtaining survey data. It shares many of the advantages of the interview in tapping psychological data such as attitudes and opinions. It can address behavioral intentions, help to anticipate reactions to future events, and provide explanations for events. It also allows workers to respond anonymously to very sensitive or personal questions that they would not be willing to discuss with an interviewer. Usually, data collection can be done more efficiently by the questionnaire than by the interview. A forty-five-minute questionnaire can often produce as much information as a two-hour interview.

The questionnaire, however, does not possess the flexibility of the interview. The interview can be used to thoroughly investigate an issue and to pursue unanticipated issues; questionnaires must anticipate such issues or ignore them. But its very rigidity does provide a standardized method of data collection. Variations in an interviewer's style from person to person may influence the data that the interviewer receives. A questionnaire reduces this kind of error by presenting the same questions to each respondent in the same way.

Questionnaires can be subject to a series of response biases:

1) A "social desirability" tendency causes a respondent to give an answer which is perceived as socially acceptable;
2) "Acquiescence" tendencies produce answers which agree (or conversely disagree) with all or most questions;
3) "Extremity" biases result in a tendency to use or avoid extremes in responding.

To the extent that people differ in these biases, the resulting data will be less valid. Thus, the construction of valid, reliable questionnaires with few response bias problems has received considerable attention from researchers and practitioners alike. In Chapter Four we discuss several instruments which have accomplished this quite well and which, in turn, can provide some guidance for the construction of questionnaires.

The unique strengths and weaknesses of both interviews and questionnaires suggest that a combination of the two techniques provides the most effective organizational survey program. Thus, selective preliminary interviewing can be helpful for identifying critical issues to include in a comprehensive questionnaire. In addition, follow-up interviews can be useful for probing deeper into critical areas assessed by the questionnaire. This later interview can renew the cycle by identifying new issues to include in subsequent questionnaires.

Whatever the approach or combination of approaches, one of the valuable functions of the survey process is to describe the overall feeling of a group rather than the select or atypical opinions of its most outspoken members. But it can describe both typical and atypical situations. In most organizations, the survey program provides an important service for the manager who often overreacts to, or makes spurious generalizations based on, isolated opinions.

In a sense, the survey approach combines both journalistic and historical methods. Like journalists, survey practitioners report on current events (organizational conditions and problems) of immediate interest. Survey practitioners, however, are careful to avoid interpreting an isolated event as a general condition. Like historians, they interpret current events in the context of past events. That is, they place current survey results in the context of the results from surveys in the past. Although it would be naive to suggest that surveys achieve the impossible goal of providing managers with "instant history," they can furnish timely information that represents the attitudes, beliefs, and opinions of a majority of employees.

Theoretical Orientation 2

This chapter discusses four significant theories of motivation and satisfaction. It is designed primarily for the manager who wants to understand the rationale of survey approaches and the psychological basis for much of their content. Although each of these theories has limitations, each offers useful insights into the sources and consequences of job satisfaction. Maslow's need-hierarchy theory and Herzberg's two-factor theory explain motivation as a function of the satisfaction of human needs. Equity theory emphasizes the importance of social comparisons in accounting for satisfaction. Finally, expectancy theory asserts that the combination of expectancy, instrumentality, and valence values determines motivation.

NEED HIERARCHY THEORY

Maslow's well-known need hierarchy theory is based on the assertion that people are motivated by their desire to satisfy a set of universal needs. These needs are physiological or survival,

FIGURE 2.1   Maslow's Need Hierarchy.

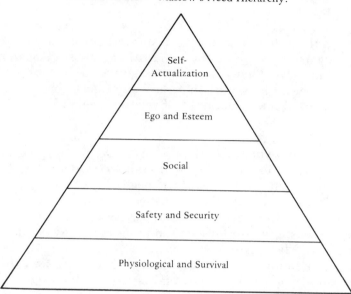

safety and security, social, ego or self-esteem, and self-actualization. According to Maslow (1943, 1965), a need which remains
largely unsatisfied causes a person to act to satisfy that need.
Once the need is satisfied, it should have little additional power
to motivate or satisfy the person. To use a simplified example:
people stranded in the desert are highly motivated to satisfy their
need for water. After they find a water supply and consume
enough water to satisfy the need, however, they are no longer
motivated to seek water. They cannot derive any more satisfaction from more water at that point. It is possible, however, for
water to become a motivating force if the need becomes manifest
again.

    According to the theory, there is a particular order in
which people will generally strive to satisfy these needs. To
quote Maslow:

    It is quite true that man lives by bread alone—when there
    is no bread. But what happens to man's desires when

there is plenty of bread and when his belly is chronically filled?

At once, other (and "higher") needs emerge and these, rather than physiological hungers, dominate the organism. And when these in turn are satisfied, again new (and still "higher") needs emerge and so on. This is what we mean by saying that the basic human needs are organized into a hierarchy of relative prepotency (1943, p. 375).

Individuals strive to satisfy their lowest order needs (physiological and survival) in the hierarchy first; higher order needs do not become important until these basic needs have been adequately satisfied. Once they have been fulfilled, they will cease to motivate or to increase satisfaction. The person will continue in this manner, focusing on the lowest need in the hierarchy that has not been adequately satisfied.

The implications of this theory for organizations should be obvious. In order to motivate and satisfy employees, organizations should offer outcomes that are consistent with workers' current or emerging needs. Thus, a discussion of each need seems appropriate.

Physiological needs

These are the basic needs in Maslow's theory. Because these needs are satisfied for most employees of American organizations, they have little effect on workers' motivation. If a person's food supply is cut off, however, food is likely to become a very important need. During the winter of 1978, for example, many miners had trouble providing food for their families because of the length of the United Mine Workers' strike. It has been said that a major reason for the miners' approval of the final settlement was the need to get food back on their tables. In fact, one of the levers used by the government to help achieve a settlement was the denial of food stamps to miners who defied a Taft-Hartley injunction. But early in the strike when most miners still had food stockpiled, there was very little talk about any physiological needs—workers were apparently motivated by very different needs.

Safety and security needs

Today, organizations meet many of the safety needs of their members reasonably well. These include the need for job security and a retirement income; medical and dental insurance; and unemployment and disability benefits. To the extent that these needs are still active, however, organizational policies and benefits that address them should be satisfying and motivating.

Social needs

Maslow originally referred to these as love needs. This group encompasses the need for emotional love, for friends, and for affectionate relationships with people in general. This set of needs is always present to some extent and can be fulfilled in any organizational setting in which more than one person works. In organizations it is usually served by human relations programs and other socially oriented supervisory practices. Often, however, organizations encourage the fulfillment of these needs during nonwork hours rather than in the workplace. As a result, a good deal of potential work-related motivation is lost.

Esteem needs

All people in our society . . . have a need or desire for a stable, firmly based, (usually) high evaluation of themselves, for self-respect or self-esteem, and for the esteem of others. By firmly based self-esteem we mean that which is soundly based upon real capacity, achievement, and respect from others (Maslow, 1943, p. 381).

Esteem needs can often be satisfied in organizations if organizations and tasks are properly designed. In fact, by satisfying these needs, an organization is helping its employees to meet its own needs as well, since an individual worker's achievement normally benefits the organization. These needs seem to be rapidly emerging among the highly educated members of the present work force, who have high expectations regarding the meaningfulness of work.

Self-actualization

This is the highest order need in Maslow's hierarchy. It becomes prepotent when all others have been reasonably well satisfied. Self-actualization is the desire for self-fulfillment—becoming what one is capable of becoming. According to Maslow, this need can never be satisfied. In fact, our observation confirms his view that relatively few people even reach this level of the hierarchy. The definition of this need suggests that realization of one's full potential can be motivating and satisfying to the employee and beneficial to the organization. For a person with manifest self-actualization needs, however, a job of limited scope will probably motivate that person to achieve self-actualization through means other than work. This could lead to reduced attention to the job or withdrawal from the organization.

There has been support for some of Maslow's arguments and for some closely related ideas, although the complete theory has not been adequately tested. A paper by Lawler and Suttle (1972) discusses much of the supporting research and suggests a simpler model of need satisfaction. They conclude that the data would best fit a two-level hierarchy with the basic biological and safety needs constituting the lower level and all other needs grouped as the upper level. Their research also indicates that individual preferences for the higher order needs differ substantially.

Maslow's theory and motivational strategies

It is interesting to note that Maslow's model seems to summarize, in chronological order, the stages through which industrial motivation strategies have passed. Thus, it offers some insight into possible future developments. The earliest attempts to motivate workers or to provide even a primitive sense of job satisfaction were directed at the lower levels of human needs. The fact that these approaches worked was probably due to the salience of these needs at the time. For example, the early efforts to organize workers were based almost solely on providing a sense of job security. Early employment legislation (e.g., factory safety regulations, child labor laws, etc.) attempted to provide minimal guarantees of basic physiological, safety, and security needs.

Even the work of Frederick W. Taylor (the father of scientific management) and others can be viewed, at least in part, as an effort to give workers a greater chance to satisfy basic needs. During the first several decades of this century, the satisfaction of these lower needs was reinforced by additional employment legislation, the rapid growth of unions, and the introduction of many corporate benefit programs. As these needs were satisfied, they became less important and less powerful as bases for motivating workers.

In the late 1920s a new need—the social need—was "discovered." Starting with the Hawthorne studies (the main catalyst of the Human Relations movement), advocates claimed that it was the "sole and sovereign" need of workers. With this contention, the Human Relations approach to worker motivation began in earnest. After several decades of very dramatic results, interest in this approach also seemed to wane as many authors apparently became skeptical of its value. It may well be that social needs lost their motivating power because the Human Relations movement succeeded too well. For a whole generation, employees have expected a humane approach from management and have accepted good human relations as a condition of work rather than a novel incentive. In other words, the desire for social need satisfaction on the job has been rather fully satisfied. As a result, it too has little motivational impact.

Within the last decade, the concept of work enrichment has been "proposed" as the definitive answer to worker motivation. This idea appeals to the esteem needs as well as to the survival, security, and social needs of the worker. As Maslow predicted, these needs have emerged as the other more basic needs have been satisfied. Today we are experiencing a whole series of moves to upgrade the challenge of work and to increase workers' feelings of responsibility in their work. Programs for improving the technical skills of workers at all levels of an organization are flourishing. Because ego needs will probably not be satisfied as readily as the lower level needs, their motivational impact may last for some time. Thus, organizations would be well advised to concentrate on programs that appeal to these needs.

The Maslow model also points the way toward the next stage of development. Programs designed to satisfy self-actualizing needs allow the workers greater freedom in the workplace. However, these are relatively few in number and not widely used. The recent movement toward improvement in the quality of work life is also a step in this direction. It appears that organizations interested in creating or maintaining high levels of motivation must be sensitive to the existing and emerging needs of workers.

TWO-FACTOR THEORY

Frederick Herzberg's two-factor (motivation-hygiene) theory has received more attention during the past two decades than any other single theory of motivation and satisfaction. The impact of Herzberg's work in this area has been tremendous and will probably continue to be important. Perhaps its most important contribution to the field has been its catalytic effect in stimulating a great deal of research into satisfaction and motivation.

The basic theory (Herzberg, Mausner, and Snyderman, 1959) suggests that people have two sets of needs. The first set involves the avoidance of "pain"; the second set involves the pursuit of psychological growth. Extrinsic factors ("hygiene factors") are not specifically related to an individual's job. These include company policies, supervision, salary, job security, and working conditions. They correspond to the need to avoid "pain" and are the primary determinants of job dissatisfaction. On the other hand, intrinsic factors ("motivators") such as achievement, recognition, the quality of the work, and responsibility correspond to the need for psychological growth. These are the main sources of job motivation or satisfaction. Herzberg implies that only the second set of factors (motivators) is capable of motivating employees to perform. Obviously, the implications of this theory for organizational control are profound, since a factor such as money would not be effective in motivating employees according to the theory.

The original theory was based on a study of 203 accountants and engineers (Herzberg et al., 1959). These workers were asked to describe critical incidents that were particularly satisfying and others that were especially dissatisfying. An analysis of the content of these incidents, shown in Table 2.1, revealed that satisfying events consisted primarily of intrinsic (motivator)

TABLE 2.1   Percentage of Good and Bad Critical Incidents in Which
Each Factor Appeared.

Factor	Percentage*	
	Good	Bad
Achievement (M)	41†	7
Recognition (M)	33†	18
Work (M)	26†	14
Responsibility (M)	23†	6
Advancement (M)	20†	11
Salary (H)	15	17
Possibility of growth (M)	6	8
Interpersonal relations—subordinate (H)	6	3
Status (H)	4	4
Interpersonal relations—superior (H)	4	15†
Interpersonal relations—peers (H)	3	8†
Supervision—technical (H)	3	20†
Company policy and administration (H)	3	31†
Working conditions (H)	1	11†
Personal life (H)	1	6†
Job security (H)	1	1
Percentage of total contributed by Ms	78	36
Percentage of total contributed by Hs	22	64

Source: Herzberg et al. (1959).
Note: Abbreviations are M = motivator, H = hygiene.
*The percentages total more than 100% since more than one job factor can be mentioned in a single critical incident.
†The difference between the percentage of good and bad critical incidents is significant at the .01 level.

factors while dissatisfying events consisted mostly of extrinsic (hygiene) factors. Based on his analysis, Herzberg proposed two independent dimensions for job satisfaction—one relating to satisfaction and one to dissatisfaction. These were not represented as opposite ends of one continuum but as two separate dimensions.

Herzberg and others have cited considerable evidence in support of the two-factor theory. But critics have questioned both the method used to generate support for the theory and the research. Vroom (1964) claimed that the critical-incident method of testing the theory was at least partly responsible for the results. He argued that human defense processes lead people to attribute causes of satisfaction to their own achievements and accomplishments (e.g., work quality) but to attribute causes of dissatisfaction to factors of the work environment (e.g., supervision) over which they have little control. He further notes that tests of the theory that did not follow Herzberg's exact methods have generally provided little support.

House and Wigdor (1967) asserted that procedural deficiencies in Herzberg's research design produced inaccurate results. In fact, in a reanalysis of data from seventeen samples, House and Wigdor obtained findings that were contradictory to the two-factor theory. They drew the following conclusions from their reanalysis of Herzberg's data and from other empirical research:

1) A given factor can cause job satisfaction for one person and job dissatisfaction for another person, and vice versa. . . .
2) A given factor can cause both job satisfaction and dissatisfaction in the same sample. . . .
3) Intrinsic job factors are more important to both satisfying and dissatisfying events. . . .
4) . . . the Two-Factor theory is an oversimplification of the relationship between motivation and satisfaction, and the sources of job satisfaction and dissatisfaction (House and Wigdor, 1967, pp. 386–387).

Despite the criticism and lack of support for the complete two-factor model, Herzberg's ideas have added much breadth to investigation of the sources of satisfaction in organizations. Much of the two-factor theory is still useful if we keep in mind 1) that individual differences exist beyond those anticipated by Herzberg and 2) that most environmental factors can produce satisfaction or dissatisfaction. Herzberg's work can help managers to identify the critical dimensions of the work environment that should be assessed in order to understand worker satisfaction and to take corrective action.

EQUITY THEORY

Although there have been a number of equity theory formulations, Adams' model (1963, 1965) has received the most attention in organizations. Our discussion, therefore, is based primarily on that model. Equity theory attempts to explain satisfaction with outcomes and to predict changes in behavior (i.e., motivation to behave in a particular manner). It is based on the perceptions of the worker and on the social comparisons involved in the perception process. That is, it asserts that individuals evaluate their own circumstances by comparing them to others' circumstances.

According to equity theory, four different perceptions may influence an individual's evaluation of a situation:

1) the person's perceptions of his or her own inputs to the situation (I_p);
2) the person's perceptions of the inputs of comparison other to the situation (I_o);
3) the person's perceptions of his or her own outcomes (O_p);
4) the person's perceptions of the outcomes (O_o) of comparison other.

It is very important to note that each of these four factors is a *perception*. Also note that, for the purposes of equity theory, it is not important whether a person's perceptions are accurate or inaccurate; people will act on their subjective perceptions of a situation regardless of the objective reality of the situation. A person's perceived inputs (I_p) consist of whatever the person believes to be relevant inputs. On the job these inputs could include work effort, age, education, seniority, sex, or anything else that the person believes should influence the value of the job. A person may consider a factor such as sex to be an important input even though the organization or someone else does not.

A person's perceived outcomes (O_p) consist of factors resulting from a given situation that the person perceives as relevant and valued. Outcomes often include things such as pay, fringe benefits, and job status. It is possible that an organization could provide an outcome that the worker does not perceive or does not consider important. The worker may not be aware of employer contributions to Social Security, for example. When this occurs, that outcome will not affect the worker's evaluation of the situation. (It should be noted that the need theories discussed earlier can be used to explain the values associated with each outcome.)

The remaining two factors in equity theory are the person's perceptions about the inputs and outcomes of the comparison other (I_o and O_o). The "comparison other" could be one person (e.g., a co-worker, a supervisor, a friend, etc.), several people (e.g., workers at another plant, workers on another shift, etc.), a more abstract combination of people, an "ideal" person, or even the perceiving person at an earlier time.

According to equity theory, a person will examine two ratios:

1) $\dfrac{O_p}{I_p}$—the ratio of the person's perceived outcomes to perceived inputs, and

2) $\dfrac{O_o}{I_o}$—the ratio of the person's perceptions of the comparison person's outcomes to the comparison person's inputs.

The individual then compares these two ratios. When this comparison is made, one of the following three conditions will occur.

$$\frac{O_p}{I_p} = \frac{O_o}{I_o}$$

This equation represents a state of perceived equity. Equity theory suggests that individuals are satisfied with this condition and try to maintain it. To have a state of equity requires only that the person perceive the two ratios as equal. Thus, a person could experience a state of equity when receiving fewer outcomes than the comparison other as long as the person thought that the comparison other had proportionately higher inputs. A state of perceived equity could be beneficial for the organization if current performance levels were adequate and therefore desirable to maintain. It is likely that these performance levels could be maintained by maintaining the outcome levels.

$$\frac{O_p}{I_p} < \frac{O_o}{I_o}$$

This relationship reflects a state of inequity. In this case the person perceives insufficient outcomes or excessive inputs in reference to the comparison other. Equity theory suggests that individuals are dissatisfied with this condition and strive for a state of perceived equity. To obtain equity, people may do one or more of the following things:

1) *Decrease inputs.* To reach a state of perceived equity, people can simply lower their inputs. If workers reduce work inputs, the organization may suffer.

2) *Increase outcomes.* To reach a state of perceived equity in this situation, workers often request a pay increase. This would require the organization to pay more for the same amount of work.

3) *Distort inputs and/or outcomes cognitively.* This would require no actual change in either inputs or outcomes but merely changes in the person's perceptions. This can be encouraged by the organization through feedback and training. It could involve upgrading the value of the comparison other's inputs ("Joe Smith is doing more work than I used to realize"); downgrading the comparison other's outcomes ("Joe Smith probably doesn't get paid as much as I used to think"); upgrading the person's perceived outcomes ("the value of my retirement benefits is actually greater than I used to realize"); or downgrading the person's perceived inputs ("I guess my work isn't really very good").

4) *Leave the situation.* This could entail quitting the job, obtaining a transfer, or increasing absenteeism. None of these choices is likely to be good for the organization.

5) *Act on other.* A worker might attempt to get the comparison other to leave the organization, which generally would be bad for the organization. Or, a worker might encourage the comparison other to raise his or her inputs, which could be very good for the organization.

6) *Change comparison other.* With this solution the person simply decides that it would be better to choose

a new comparison other with whom he or she is
more likely to be in a state of equity. It is possible
for a manager to encourage a worker to choose a
more "reasonable" comparison person.

$$\frac{O_p}{I_p} > \frac{O_o}{I_o}$$

Under this condition a state of inequity also exists because people feel that their outcomes are too high in reference to
the comparison other. Any of the six types of changes used to
reduce the state of inequity discussed above could also be used in
this situation. However, people are relatively tolerant of this sort
of perceived inequity: managers seldom hear workers complain
that they are overpaid! If this form of inequity becomes great
enough, however, the person will tend to be dissatisfied (i.e.,
experience guilt) and act to reduce the inequity. It is usually best
for the organization if this is accomplished through an increase in
inputs.

Adams (1965) proposed that the following set of proposi-
tions would influence a person's choice among the various
methods for reducing inequity:

a) Person will maximize positively valent [valued]
   outcomes . . . .
b) Person will minimize increasing inputs that are
   effortful and costly to change.
c) Person will resist real and cognitive changes in inputs that are central to self-concept and to self-esteem. To the extent that any one Person's outcomes
   are related to self-concept and to self-esteem, this
   proposition is extended to cover outcomes.
d) Person will be more resistant to changing cognitions about his/her own outcomes and inputs than
   to changing cognitions about Other's outcomes and
   inputs.
e) Leaving the field will be resorted to only when the
   magnitude of inequity experienced is high and
   other means of reducing it are unavailable. Partial

withdrawal, such as absenteeism, will occur more frequently and under conditions of lower inequity.

f) Person will be highly resistant to changing the object of comparisons. A comparison Other, once it has stabilized over time . . . , in effect, has become an anchor (pp. 295–96).

Equity theory is intuitively appealing to many and has received a considerable amount of attention. A substantial amount of research has been devoted to testing Adams' equity theory. Goodman and Friedman (1971) examined much of the empirical evidence that was used to test the theory. They concluded that several equity theory components received fairly strong empirical support. The evidence substantiated the idea that perceived inequity is a source of tension and that the drive to reduce this tension increases as the amount of inequity increases. It also showed that comparisons of input/outcome ratios are a source of perceived inequity and therefore dissatisfaction. In addition, the research indicated rather clearly that people tend to be less reactive to "overpayment" than to "underpayment." Finally, it demonstrated that people prefer to maximize their positive outcomes when this can reduce perceived inequity.

Another set of equity theory ideas has received at least tentative empirical support. For example, people apparently do resist changing their perceptions of inputs or outcomes if they are central to the person's self-concept. People also resist changing their comparison other once he or she has become a referent.

Investigation of the relationship between equity and compensation systems reveals that "overpaid" *hourly* workers attempt to reduce inequity by producing at a relatively high level. On the other hand, "overpaid" *piece-rate* workers tend to produce less quantity but higher quality than equitably paid workers. Finally, "underpaid" *hourly* workers tend to invest lower inputs than workers who feel that they are equitably paid.

Equity theory provides some valuable insights into the determinants of satisfaction and motivation. The principles of the theory demand that organizations (and surveys) address themselves not only to workers' inputs and outcomes but also to available social comparisons. It is often possible for an organization to influence critical worker perceptions by making explicit the inputs required for rewards. When this is done, the management task is simplified because workers tend to share many perceptions. It is important to note that the worker can reduce inequity in several ways. The skilled manager, aware of these alternatives, can help the worker choose an approach that is good for the worker and for the organization.

EXPECTANCY THEORY

There have been several different versions of expectancy theory presented in recent years. This complex theory represents a model of motivation in organizations; however, its scope extends beyond our application of it in this book. We use expectancy theory to explain a process by which workers obtain satisfaction in organizations. The model also identifies a number of critical factors that influence worker satisfaction and organizational effectiveness.[1]

Figure 2.2, adapted from the Porter and Lawler model (1968), shows the relationship among the components of expectancy theory. According to the theory, three factors influence the probability that a person will choose to perform in a particular manner: expectancy (E→P), instrumentality (P→O), and valence (V) (these terms are discussed in more detail below). The combination of these three factors determines the person's motivation to engage in a particular act. In general, the more positive the value of these three factors for a given act, the more likely the person is to try to behave in that manner. In fact, the following specific combination of these factors has been proposed as an indication of the total force (motivation) to behave in a particular manner:

$$\text{FORCE} = \Sigma \left[(E{\to}P) \times \Sigma \left[(P{\to}O) \times (V) \right] \right]$$

The highest force score results when workers perceive a very high probability that their effort will lead to successful perfor-

1. *Our presentation is based primarily on a model by Porter and Lawler (1968), but we will make several modifications. The interested reader in search of a more detailed treatment of the theory would be well advised to read the Porter and Lawler (1968) book, a book by Vroom (1964), an article by Mitchell and Biglan (1971), and an article by Schwab and Cummings (1970).*

FIGURE 2.2 Modified Porter and Lawler Model.

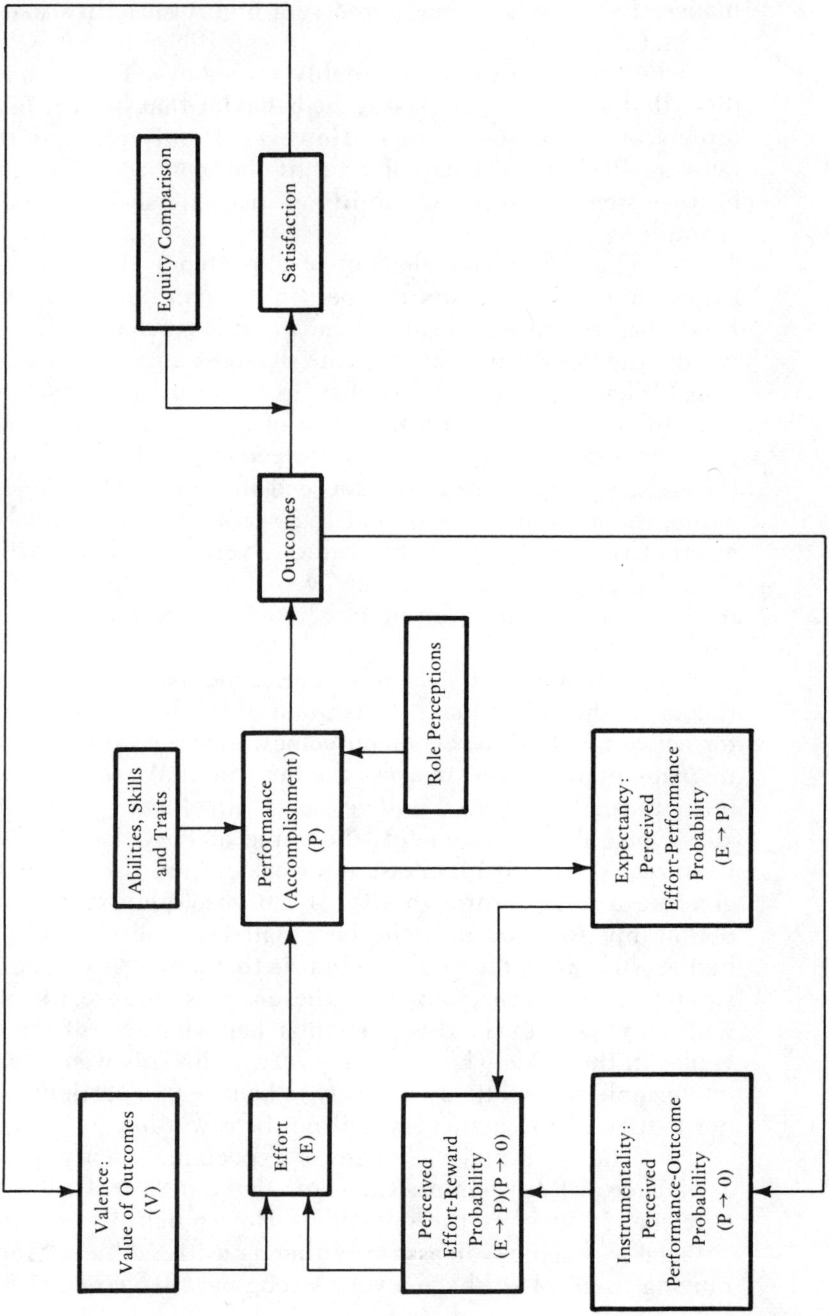

mance (E→P), when they perceive a high probability that this successful performance will lead to specific outcomes (P→O), and when these outcomes are highly valued (V). The theory predicts that a person will choose the behavior that has the highest force score associated with it. However, it only predicts that a person will *attempt* a particular act; it does not predict the probability of success. Necessary ability to succeed may be lacking, for example.

The first major element of expectancy theory is called expectancy. It represents the person's perception of the likelihood that effort will lead to the intended behavior. In other words, the E→P expectancy is the person's answer to the question, "What is the probability that if I try I can do it?" Since this is a probability statement, the value of E→P can range from zero ("There is no possible way I can succeed even if I try") through 1 ("I am absolutely sure I will succeed if I try"). The higher the value, the more likely it is that the person will be motivated to attempt this behavior. If this value is zero, the person will not choose this particular behavior even if the other values in the model (P→O, V) are very high. This would explain why people seldom set goals for themselves that they consider unattainable.

Instrumentality (P→O), the second major element of the theory, is the individual's perception of the likelihood that performance will lead to certain outcomes. In other words, the P→O instrumentality value answers the question, "What is the probability that if I succeed, I will get something for it?" Since this is also a probability statement, the value of P→O can also range from zero ("Even if I increase my work output, the boss will not give me a raise") through 1.0 ("I am absolutely sure that if I double my work output, the boss will give me a raise"). The higher this value, the more likely it is that a person will be motivated to behave a certain way. If these values are zero, the person will not choose to try this particular behavior even if the other values in the model (E→P, V) are very high. This would explain why people are relatively unlikely to behave in a particular manner if they feel that success will not be rewarded.

The third major element of expectancy theory is known as valence (V). It is simply the value that a person attaches to an outcome. It answers the question, "How much do I value this outcome?" Valence can assume either a positive or negative value ranging from −1 ("I have a very strong negative reaction to this outcome") to zero ("I really have no feelings one way or the other about the outcome") to +1 ("I have a very strong positive reaction to this outcome"). The more positive the values, the more likely it is that a person will be motivated to achieve that outcome. On the other hand, negative values will discourage the individual from attempting to reach that outcome.

Outcomes are classified as either intrinsic or extrinsic in this model. The intrinsic outcomes—interest in the work, feeling of accomplishment, etc.—stem directly from the work itself. Since these outcomes are not dependent on other people, they are often associated with relatively high $P \rightarrow O$ perceptions. The extrinsic outcomes—pay, promotions, etc.—are given or controlled by other people. To the extent that these outcomes are poorly administered, they are often associated with relatively low $P \rightarrow O$ perceptions.

Most behaviors are associated with a series of possible outcomes. Typically, some of these outcomes have positive valence, such as a large pay raise; others have negative valences, such as fatigue from working hard; and some have essentially zero valence. For each of these outcomes, there is a perceived probability that performance will lead to that particular outcome. A worker may perceive, for example, that working overtime every night will definitely lead to fatigue ($P \rightarrow O = 1.0$) but that there is only a fifty-fifty chance that working overtime will lead to a pay raise ($P \rightarrow O = .50$).

According to expectancy theory, people combine these factors with the $E \rightarrow P$ perception in order to choose among alternative behavior possibilities. The model predicts that the person will choose to behave in whatever way has the highest motivational force resulting from these three factors.

> In the case of productivity, this means that people will be motivated to be highly productive if they feel they can be highly productive and if they see a number of positive outcomes associated with being a high producer (Lawler, 1973, p. 52).

Expectancy theory is a very complex model of human behavior that provides a good summary of many critical factors that influence behavior in organizations. Obviously, no worker sits down and writes out the $E \rightarrow P$, $P \rightarrow O$, and V values for all possible behaviors and applies the force equation in order to make decisions. It would be absurd to suggest that a manager should attempt to do the same in deciding how to manage his or her subordinates. But managers can increase E→P perceptions through training, through selection of skilled employees, and through clear goals and job definitions. They can maximize P→O perceptions by appropriate design and by adherence to pay schedules and other organizational reward policies. Finally, although it is difficult to change the values that workers attach to outcomes (V), managers can assess these values and provide the outcomes that workers desire. All of these methods are likely to increase workers' motivation to perform in the preferred manner.

Expectancy theory, therefore, is useful for several reasons. The assessment of E→P perceptions gives an indication of the effectiveness of selection and training policies. The appraisal of P→O perceptions provides an evaluation of organizational reward policies as the worker sees them. The measurement of V values identifies the outcomes that workers like or dislike. This information suggests areas in which organizational change would be effective.

As indicated earlier, there is no generally accepted theory of satisfaction or motivation. However, there are similarities among the theories discussed above. For example, the need theories focus on determinants of values of various outcomes. Equity theory deals with individuals' evaluations of valued outcomes through comparisons to their own inputs and to the inputs and outcomes of the comparison other. The Porter and Lawler model of expectancy theory bases the value of outcomes on need theory and uses a form of equity theory to explain the determinants of satisfaction. Collectively, these theories encompass the majority of human and organizational factors that influence worker behavior.

In addition, these theories provide the psychological basis for various survey approaches by identifying critical factors in the work environment that affect worker motivation and organizational effectiveness. Surveys can be designed to address these issues. They can assess whether employees' needs, as described in the Maslow and Herzberg theories, have been satisfied; they can determine whether perceived inequity exists among employees; or they can evaluate employees' motivation by measuring their E→P, P→O, and V values. Thus, despite their limitations, these theories are essential for understanding surveys and job satisfaction.

REFERENCES

Adams, J. S. Toward an understanding of inequity. *Journal of Applied Psychology,* 1963, 67:422-36.

Adams, J. S. Inequity in social exchange. *Advances in Experimental Social Psychology,* ed., L. Berkowitz, Academic Press, 1965, 276-99.

Goodman, P. S. and Friedman, A. An examination of Adams' theory of inequity, *Administrative Science Quarterly,* 1971, 16:271-88.

Herzberg, F., Mausner, B., and Snyderman, B. *The Motivation to Work,* 2d ed., Wiley, 1959.

House, R. J. and Wigdor, L. A. Herzberg's dual-factor theory of job satisfaction and motivation: A review of the evidence and a criticism. *Personnel Psychology,* 1967, 20:369-89.

Lawler, E. E., III. *Motivation in Work Organizations,* Brooks/Cole, 1973.

Lawler, E. E., III and Suttle, J. L. A causal correlational test of the need hierarchy concept. *Organizational Behavior and Human Performance,* 1972, 7:265-87.

Maslow, A. H. A theory of human motivation. *Psychological Review,* 1943, 50:370-96.

Maslow, A. H. *Eupsychian Management,* Irwin, 1965.

Mitchell, T. R. and Biglan, A. Instrumentality theories: Current uses in psychology, *Psychological Bulletin,* 1971, 76: 432-54.

Porter, L. W. and Lawler, E. E., III. *Managerial Attitudes and Performance.* Irwin-Dorsey, 1968.

Schwab, D. P. and Cummings, L. L. Theories of performance and satisfaction: A review. *Industrial Relations,* 1970, 7: 408-30.

Vroom, V. H. *Work and Motivation.* Wiley, 1964.

Organizational Surveys: 3
The Purposes

This chapter discusses several reasons for conducting organizational surveys. They are grouped into four categories: 1) feedback; 2) diagnosis; 3) communication; and 4) training. In addition, two sections at the end of the chapter explain how surveys can be used as an expression of an organization's concern for its employees and as a means of quantifying the financial impact of employee attitudes on organizational effectiveness.

FEEDBACK FUNCTION

Surveys can provide management with knowledge about the organization that is not readily available by other means. Since this information is obtained directly from workers, it should be subject to relatively small amounts of distortion if a survey is designed well. The feedback function is especially important for executives of large, decentralized organizations because it is virtually impossible for them to have any current knowledge of how policies are being administered or accepted by workers.

In one sense, surveys are analogous to the audit function. Whereas an audit provides a systematic examination of corporate records, an organizational survey provides a systematic assessment of employees' perceptions of the state of organizational health. This information can prove invaluable for organizational planning and can often reduce some of the ambiguity involved in making management decisions. For example, knowledge of worker attitudes toward various forms of compensation can aid management in designing or changing a compensation system. Similarly, knowledge of worker attitudes toward various job characteristics can help with the design or redesign of jobs.

The use of systematic surveys can sensitize the organization to changes in employee preferences or reactions over time. It can also be valuable for monitoring or evaluating workers' immediate reactions to organizational changes. By focusing attention on the "good" and "bad" aspects of changes, the survey helps the manager to "fine-tune" change procedures and to maximize the effectiveness of future changes.

In the following three examples, based on actual survey data, organizational surveys were used primarily for 1) auditing, 2) planning, and 3) assessing organizational change, respectively.

A survey as an audit device

In 1975, Sears, Roebuck, and Company conducted a survey of 784 buyers, assistant buyers, and assistant sales managers from eight units of the corporate branch of the company. It was designed to measure the executives' satisfaction with six specific elements of the work and work environment (job satisfaction facets) as well as their general job satisfaction levels. Measures were also made of critical job characteristics, organizational environment characteristics, and certain individual characteristics of these executives. Table 3.1 lists the variables included in this audit.

The results of this survey (summarized in Dunham, 1975) were used to examine the relative levels of satisfaction with different facets and to determine which of the individual, job, and organizational environment variables were related to

TABLE 3.1   Variables Included in Survey.

Job Satisfaction Facets	Individual Characteristics
1. Supervision	1. Sex
2. Career Future	2. Age
3. Financial	3. Race
4. Amount of Work	4. Education Level
5. Kind of Work	5. Company Tenure
6. Company Policies and Practices	
7. Overall Satisfaction	

Job Characteristics	Organizational Environment Characteristics
1. Task Significance	1. Company Support Level
2. Skill Variety	2. Leadership: Interpersonal Orientation
3. Task Identity	3. Leadership: Task Orientation
4. Autonomy	4. Work-Assignment Favorableness
5. Task Feedback	5. Career Favorableness
	6. Organizational Climate
	7. Work-Group Climate

these satisfaction levels. Figure 3.1 summarizes the overall relationships of these sets of variables to the job satisfaction variables. On the average, individual characteristics accounted for only 2 percent of the variation in job satisfaction scores while job characteristics and organizational environment characteristics explained 12 percent and 38 percent of the variation, respectively.

The Sears analysis provided some important observations:

1) Of the individual characteristics, only tenure and age were related to any of the satisfaction variables and even these were related only to satisfaction with career future and with company policies and practices. Older workers with longer tenure with the company were more satisfied than were younger, newer employees.

2) All five job characteristic variables were related to the job satisfaction variables. By far the strongest relationship was between job characteristics and

satisfaction with the kind of work. In general, as the significance, variety, identity, autonomy, and feedback perceived in a job increased, satisfaction with the kind of work increased also—as did, to a lesser extent, satisfaction with supervision and satisfaction with company policies and practices.

3) All organizational environment characteristics were related to one or more job satisfaction variables. Satisfaction with supervision and career future had the strongest relationships to organizational variables while satisfaction with financial aspects and with amount of work had the weakest relationships. Organizational and work-group climate both had a positive impact on satisfaction with company policies and practices. Company support level positively influenced satisfaction with career future more than any other variable. Both interpersonal and task-oriented leadership behavior were very strongly related to satisfaction with supervision. Descriptions of current work assignments were highly related to satisfaction with

FIGURE 3.1   Average Amount of Predicted Job Satisfaction Variance.

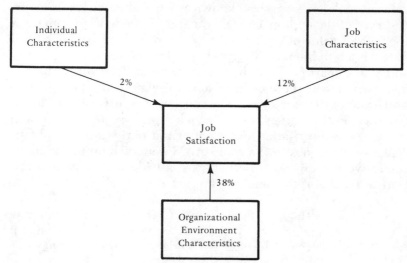

the kind of work. Finally, positive descriptions of the career were indicative of satisfaction with career future and with company policies and practices.

Although these data cannot prove cause-effect relationships, they do provide a comprehensive overview of the current state of the organization. Such a perspective is valuable for understanding the interaction of employees, jobs, and elements of the organization.

A survey as a planning tool

In 1977 and 1978, Integrity Mutual, a small midwestern insurance company, surveyed forty-three employees, from the first-level supervisor to the president (see Dunham, 1978). The primary purpose of the survey was to help the company make decisions about the design for a new compensation plan. Workers were asked to describe the various duties that their jobs required, their perceptions of performance-reward contingencies, and their satisfaction with their pay. Supervisors of each job also described the job requirements for these employees.

Using results of this survey, an estimate of the relative value of each job—a process known as job evaluation—was made. A survey of the appropriate labor market provided an estimate of the market value of each job. By comparing the actual pay level for each job to the relative job value (determined by the survey) and to the market value, it was possible to determine whether discrepancies in these comparisons influenced the job satisfaction levels of the employees. The concept of equity was applied in two ways in this survey. First, the job inputs (requirements) and outcomes (compensation) were compared to the inputs and outcomes of other jobs in the company. Second, job inputs and outcomes were compared to other jobs outside the company. The critical results of this analysis are listed below:

1) Although there was a wide range in actual pay among jobs, there was only a weak relationship between level of pay and satisfaction with pay.

2) There was a strong, relationship between perceptions of performance-reward contingencies and
satisfaction with pay. Satisfaction with pay was
significantly higher for workers who felt that their
level of pay was a function of their performance
level, even if their level of pay was relatively low.
Apparently, they were satisfied as long as their low
level of pay reflected their own relatively low level
of performance.

3) Discrepancies in pay among jobs in the company
had a moderately strong influence on satisfaction
with pay. Workers who felt that they were underpaid in comparison to other employees in the company (considering the various job requirements or
inputs) had relatively low levels of satisfaction
with pay.

4) For lower-level employees, satisfaction with pay
was not significantly influenced by comparisons to
jobs outside the company. Apparently, these comparisons were not made or were not considered important by these employees.

5) For managers at the highest levels of the company,
however, comparisons to jobs outside the company
did have a significant influence on satisfaction with
pay. Managers who felt underpaid in comparison to
managers with similar jobs in other companies had
relatively low levels of satisfaction with pay.

The results of this survey were very useful for planning
the new compensation system. Because of the importance of
strong performance-reward contingencies, a compensation program based on merit was instituted. To support this decision, a
comprehensive system was designed to appraise performance.
Organizational policy was modified to encourage effective use of
the merit-based compensation system. Because of the importance
of job comparisons within the company, the new compensation
structure was based on the relative level of worker requirements
for each job. In view of the importance of managers' comparisons
of their jobs to similar jobs at other companies, adjustments to the
salary structure were made to reduce inequitable comparisons. It

is too soon to evaluate the effects of these changes, but the initial survey results can now serve as a basis of comparison for future evaluative surveys.

A survey to assess organizational changes

In 1975 and 1976, surveys were conducted in two branches of a large insurance company (see Dunham, Newman, and Blackburn, 1978). The organization's executives had decided to replace a paper-record file system used by clerical and semitechnical workers with a computerized microfiche system, but they were concerned that increases in technological efficiency might be counterbalanced by negative worker responses to the new system. Thus, the purpose of the survey was to determine whether the introduction of this automated system would cause changes in worker attitudes.

The 118 employees involved in the survey were divided into two groups. A control group of 75 employees from one division of the regional office used the old filing system. An experimental group of 43 employees from another division of the same regional office used the new system. A survey questionnaire was administered to both groups of employees one week before the new system was installed. Three months after the change another questionnaire was administered to both groups.

The survey attempted to measure employee satisfaction with the work, with job involvement, and with motivation from the work itself. It evaluated employees' intentions to be absent or to resign as well as attitudes toward absenteeism and resignation. Finally, it assessed perceived job complexity (a combination of variety, autonomy, identity, significance, and feedback). In all cases, employees voluntarily provided individual identification for follow-up purposes.

The control group provided a comparison standard and eliminated many possible incorrect explanations of the results. For example, if some factor other than the technological change influenced the responses of the experimental group, this extraneous factor might have been falsely interpreted as an effect of the technological change. Most extraneous factors, however, would also influence the control group since the two groups were highly similar. Thus, the organization wanted to know if there were changes in the experimental group that did not occur for the control group.

The results of this series of surveys showed that there were no significant changes in the average responses of the experimental group to questions about satisfaction, motivation, or behavioral intentions after the introduction of the new microfiche system. Furthermore, the average responses of the experimental group were not significantly different from those of the control group. Thus, on the average, the anticipated negative effects of the change did not occur.

Another interesting result was detected, however, upon a closer examination of the data. Although on the average there were no significant effects, many workers did perceive changes in job complexity. Because some workers perceived an increase while others perceived a decrease in complexity, there was no average change. The fact that more of these changes occurred in the experimental group than in the control group suggested that the new system did have some effect. Furthermore, those people who perceived decreases in the complexity of the job became less satisfied with the work, less motivated by the work, and more likely to resign. These negative effects were offset by persons who perceived increases in complexity. They became more satisfied with the work, more motivated by the work, and less likely to resign.

Overall, the results of these surveys indicated that the introduction of the new filing system would have inconsistent effects on workers. The company could proceed to install the system, knowing that it would probably not have major impact on average worker responses. Because some employees would probably react negatively to these changes, however, the organization would have to be prepared to deal with these individual cases.

DIAGNOSTIC FUNCTION

Surveys can serve an important diagnostic function for organizations. That is, they can explain or predict critical organizational events such as turnover, absenteeism, tardiness, union activity, and possibly even productivity. Managers who understand the causes of these events may be able to influence them.

This section provides an overview of the research on the relationship between satisfaction and each of these critical organizational events.

Unfortunately, many organizations fail to exploit the predictive value of surveys by using them only to diagnose a problem after it has emerged. It is of course quite legitimate to use organizational surveys to solve problems and to address questions such as:

1) Why are our workers dissatisfied with their pay?
2) How can we increase satisfaction with supervision?
3) How can we reduce turnover?
4) Why did our employees form a union?

It is also possible, however, to use surveys to prevent such problems or at least to identify them before they erupt into a crisis. For example, early detection of employee dissatisfaction with compensation or with company policies could permit a careful evaluation of these policies and their impact on employees *before* a union action is required. By identifying many employee concerns at a relatively early stage, surveys allow management to work toward maintaining organizational "well-being" rather than fighting to remove "illness."

The three basic potential problems that diagnostic surveys can identify require different kinds of solutions. The first type is relatively simple to solve: it requires only a "snap of management's fingers." The washroom that needs painting, the machine that needs repair, or the thermostat that needs adjustment are examples of this type of problem. The hardest part of solving these kinds of problems is often simply identifying them. The second type requires policy changes to obtain solutions. These may be as simple as a change in the dress code or as complex as a change in organizational structure. The third type necessitates the creative efforts of both management and employees to solve because there are no prescribed solutions.

In the following overview, we examine a number of organizational problems: turnover, absenteeism, union activity, and low levels of performance. As stated earlier, managers who use surveys to obtain information about these problems may be able to minimize their negative effects.

Turnover

In the past twenty-five years there have been four classic reviews of the relationship of turnover to job satisfaction (Brayfield and Crockett, 1955; Herzberg, Mausner, Peterson, and Capwell, 1957; Vroom, 1964; and Porter and Steers, 1973). The results of these reviews have been fairly consistent in showing that there is an inverse relationship between satisfaction and turnover. This research has demonstrated that workers who have relatively low levels of job satisfaction are the most likely to quit their jobs and that organizational units with the lowest average satisfaction levels tend to have the highest turnover rates.

Figure 3.2 shows the Heneman and Schwab model (1975) of turnover theory, which is based on the March and Simon model (1958). According to the theory, the decision to quit the organization is based on perceived desirability of leaving and on perceived ease of movement. Desirability of leaving is primarily a function of job satisfaction but is also influenced by opportunities for transfer or promotion within the company. Thus, low satisfaction and few opportunities for movement within the company will make movement out of the company more desirable to the worker. Perceived ease of movement to other organizations depends on the availability of opportunities for such movement. This availability is, in turn, a function of the general level of business activity, the number of organizations that the worker views as possible job sources, the worker's level of skill. The greater the perceived ease of movement, the more likely it is that the worker will leave the company.

The two main factors in this model can be restated as: (1) Does the worker want to leave? and (2) Does the worker have anywhere else to go? Note that satisfaction should thus have its greatest impact on turnover under conditions in which perceived ease of movement is high. Heneman and Schwab concluded that "By piecing together the evidence . . . there appears to be substantial support for many March and Simon hypotheses" (p. 18).

Table 3.2 contains a summary of the relationship between overall job satisfaction and turnover from fifteen studies reviewed by Porter and Steers (1973). It is important to note that these studies included different groups of employees, such as clerical workers, salesmen, manual workers, managers, and even

FIGURE 3.2   Turnover Theory.

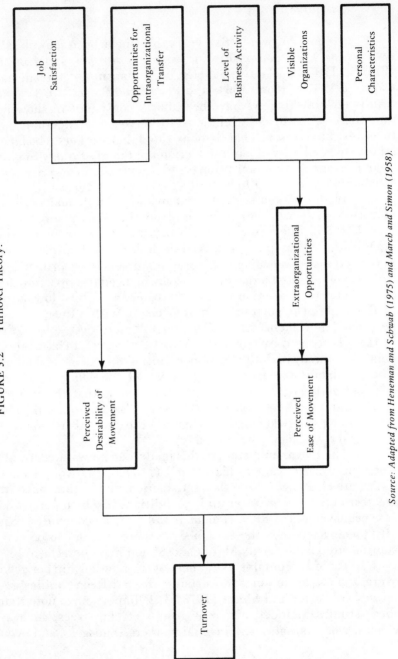

Source: Adapted from Heneman and Schwab (1975) and March and Simon (1958).

TABLE 3.2   Relation of Satisfaction to Turnover.

Employee Population	Sample Size	Relation of Satisfaction to Turnover
Insurance agents	990	Negative
Insurance agents	474	Negative
Departmental workers	NA	None
Insurance salesmen	NA	Negative
Female clerical workers	129	Negative
Female clerical workers	298	Negative
Student nurses	1852	Negative
Officer workers	660	Negative
Lower level managers	1020	Negative
Military academy cadets	1160	Negative
Retail store employees	475	Negative
Computer salesmen	Varied	Negative
Female manual workers	236	Negative
Female clerical workers	160	Negative
Air Force pilots	52	Negative

Source: Adapted from Porter and Steers (1973).
Note: NA = not available.

Air Force pilots. Each of these studies possessed methodological rigor, virtually all actually predicted turnover, and most used sound measures of job satisfaction. Thus, these findings should be reliable. An examination of Table 3.2 reveals that in fourteen of fifteen studies, significant negative relationships were found between job satisfaction and turnover.

Other studies reviewed by Porter and Steers (1973) focused on specific organization, work unit, job, and individual factors as they related to employee turnover. In eight of ten studies involving over three thousand workers from a wide variety of jobs, satisfaction with pay and promotion had significant negative relationships with turnover. In six out of seven studies that assessed satisfaction with supervision, those workers with the lowest satisfaction levels were most likely to quit their jobs, and in four out of six cases satisfaction with co-workers was negatively related to turnover. Similarly, satisfaction with job content was negatively related to turnover in all but one of nine studies. Over all, many different aspects of the work environment seemed to cause turnover.

Hulin (1966) investigated the relationship between satisfaction and turnover by sampling female clerical employees in a large manufacturing company in Montreal. We examine this study and discuss its follow-up (Hulin, 1968) to illustrate how a survey can be used both to assess and to act on a turnover problem.

Turnover among the female clerical staff at the company had averaged about 30 percent each year, compared to about 20 percent in other large companies in the area. A cost-accounting analysis showed that, at a cost of $1,000 for hiring and training each new clerical worker, direct turnover costs were $130,000 per year. Surveys were administered to 350 clerical workers to obtain basic demographic information about the workers and to assess levels of satisfaction with pay, promotion, co-workers, supervisors, the work, and the work "atmosphere."

In the six months following the survey, twenty-six of the workers who had completed the survey quit their jobs. A comparison of the satisfaction scores of the terminators and nonterminators was made, as shown in Table 3.3. A statistical test for overall differences showed that the terminators had significantly lower satisfaction scores than the nonterminators. In fact, the terminators had lower satisfaction on five of the six satisfaction facets. Because the employees who left the company were younger than most of the nonterminators, a new group of nonterminators whose ages, education, and native language matched the terminators was established. The same satisfaction differences were found when this comparison was made. A follow-up analysis

TABLE 3.3   Satisfaction Scores for Terminators and Nonterminators.

Satisfaction Facet	Nonterminators n = 319	Terminators n = 26
Work	35.87	28.69
Pay*	30.00	30.30
Promotions*	21.80	18.70
Co-workers	41.13	37.40
Supervisors	41.81	38.15
Atmosphere	34.78	32.92

Source: adapted from Hulin (1966).
*Scores adjusted for number of items.

identified another seventeen workers who quit seven to twelve months after the survey. This data revealed that the same satisfaction variables had a tendency to predict turnover as long as one year after the survey.

Following this study, the organization instituted various policy changes. After these changes were made, Hulin surveyed the company's clerical workers again. He found that satisfaction was still significantly related to turnover but that satisfaction levels had increased for four of the facets. Perhaps more importantly, the increases in satisfaction were accompanied by a decrease in turnover from 30 percent to 12 percent.

Absenteeism

The relationship between satisfaction and absenteeism (or attendance, to use a positive term) has not been investigated as thoroughly as the relationship between satisfaction and turnover. Moreover, many studies have failed to differentiate between intentional and unintentional absenteeism, illness and nonillness causes, and paid and unpaid absenteeism.[1] Despite these problems, some meaningful conclusions can be drawn. Vroom (1964) found significant relationships between satisfaction and absenteeism in seven of the nine studies that he analyzed. Porter and Steers (1973) identified significant negative relationships between overall satisfaction and absenteeism in the two recent studies they reviewed. They also found studies in which satisfaction with pay, satisfaction with co-workers, and satisfaction with job content had an impact on absenteeism. In general, it appears that various satisfaction components do influence absenteeism, but the full scope of this effect has not been well documented.

The greatest impact of job satisfaction on absenteeism should be expected under conditions where the worker is relatively free to act (see Herman, 1973) and where there are few penalties for being absent. Thus, job satisfaction is more likely to influence absenteeism for salaried employees than it is for hourly

1. *It seems important to focus on voluntary absenteeism. Unless one wishes to accept the unlikely possibility that dissatisfaction causes illness which in turn leads to absenteeism, it is futile to attempt to predict absenteeism resulting from illness with satisfaction data.*

TABLE 3.4   Correlations Between Satisfaction and Attendance.

Satisfaction Facet	Chicago†	New York
Supervision	.54**	.12
Amount of work	.36*	.01
Kind of work	.37*	.06
Pay	.46**	.11
Career future	.60**	.14
Company policies and practices	.42*	.02

Source: adapted from Smith (1977).
†Group following snowstorm.
*p < .05 (significant).
**p < .01 (highly significant).

workers. A recent study (Smith, 1977) examined a situation in which a group of salaried employees were free to attend work or to be absent on a particular day without financial penalty and without social or work-group pressures for being absent. This study involved a group of 3010 salaried employees who held various administrative, professional, and technical jobs in a company in Chicago and a second group of 340 employees who held similar jobs at the company's New York headquarters.

On April 2, 1975, an unexpected blizzard hit Chicago, greatly hampering the city's transportation system. Attendance on April 3 required not only the decision to attend, but also considerable personal effort to get to work. Attendance ranged from 39 percent to 97 percent in Chicago (Median = 70 percent) and from 89 percent to 100 percent in New York (Median = 96 percent), where no storm had occurred. (Persons absent because of travel, vacation, or prior illness were not counted.)

The correlations between group satisfaction[2] and group attendance are presented in Table 3.4. It is clear that all six satisfaction facets were significantly and strongly related to attendance in Chicago, where it was both socially and organizationally acceptable to be absent because of the snowstorm. Those groups of workers with the highest satisfaction levels were most likely to exert the high level of effort necessary to get to work. For

2. *Survey data had been collected from all of these employees in November and December of 1974. Satisfaction with supervision, amount of work, kind of work, pay, career future, and company policies and practices were assessed. Average satisfaction levels for each of twenty-seven functional groupings in Chicago and thirteen groupings in New York were calculated for this study.*

the New York group, where these conditions (permissive absenteeism) were lacking, there were no significant relationships.

Union activity

Job satisfaction can have an impact on two major aspects of union activity: (1) the tendency to form or join a union and (2) the tendency to take action within the union, such as filing grievances or striking. Traditionally, pay has been the primary consideration of union activity, but recently there has been added emphasis on medical and retirement benefits, work scheduling, and even the design of jobs. Survey data can be used to attend to critical issues that may influence union activity. This does not imply that surveys are antiunion devices. Indeed, surveys and unions have the same purpose: concern for worker needs and feelings. In fact, some union organizations often utilize surveys among their own employees and members to identify the issues that are most important to workers.

Early studies (Smith, 1962) indicated that workers who are dissatisfied with their pay or their work tend to feel more positively toward unions and are more likely to join a union. It is widely accepted now that dissatisfaction with organizational policies and practices also encourages workers to seek union assistance in correcting what they view as undesirable conditions.

Herman (1973) reported on two studies (see Getman, Goldberg, and Herman, 1976, for more complete information) of elections held to determine union representation. The first study involved an election sponsored by the Retail Clerks Association at two stores of a large discount department store chain; the second was based on an election sponsored by the United Steel Workers of America in a Chicago manufacturing company. Using structured interviews, Herman surveyed a sample of employees. She obtained measures of attitudes toward the union and measures of satisfaction with pay, hours of work, and type of work. Pre-election interviews revealed that workers with favorable attitudes toward the union and low satisfaction with the company were most likely to sign a card to authorize the election. Employees who expressed satisfaction with working conditions were not likely to support the union and in most cases voted against the unions. Using only measures of attitudes to predict how the workers would vote led to accurate predictions for 82 percent of the voters in the first study and 83 percent in the second study.

Hamner and Smith (1978) attempted to predict level of union activity by using measures of job satisfaction. A sample of 61,428 salaried employees from 188 units across the United States was studied. In 94 of these units, some union activity— from distributing handbills to losing a union election—had taken place after the administration of an attitude survey. Another 94 units, which had experienced no union activity, were chosen to match these on the basis of size, location, and function. The results indicated that 30 percent of the variance in union activity could be predicted from the measures of job satisfaction. The most important job satisfaction variable was satisfaction with supervision, although satisfaction with co-workers, career future, company policies and practices, amount of work, physical surroundings, and kind of work each had a significant impact. A study of another thirty-one units showed that these findings were consistent and to some degree generalizable.

It is not surprising to note that strikes and grievances are often a function of dissatisfaction (see Fleishman and Harris, 1962; Fleishman, Harris, and Burtt, 1955). It is important to recognize, however, that although the majority of strikes are related to wages, hours, and fringe benefits, other factors such as safety and management behavior often contribute to strike decisions as well as to the filing of grievances. Each of these factors, of course, can be evaluated by surveying employees before the grievance or strike decisions are made.

Performance

For years there has been an implicit assumption that job satisfaction influences performance. Actually, there is very little evidence to support this contention. Several reviews of the literature (e.g., Brayfield and Crockett, 1955; Herzberg, Mausner, Peterson, and Capwell, 1957; and Vroom, 1964) have analyzed a large number of studies and concluded that they fail to support a significant link between satisfaction and performance. Table 3.5, adapted from Vroom's (1964) review, presents evidence to support the idea that there is no simple relationship of satisfaction to

TABLE 3.5   Correlational Studies—Job Satisfaction and Job Performance.

Worker Population	Correlation	Type of Criterion of Productivity	N
Insurance agents	.23	Ratings	233
	.26	Objective	
Air force control tower operators	.01	Ratings	109
Hourly paid workers	.05	Ratings	890
Female office employees	.14	Ratings	231
Plumber's apprentices	.20	Ratings	55
Farmers	.12	Ratings	50
Production employees on piece work	.68	Objective	40
Work groups in an equipment manfacturing plant	−.31	Ratings	58
IBM operators	.08	Ratings	193
Departments in mail-order company	.19	Objective	25
Insurance agents	.22	Objective	552
Bus drivers	.31	Objective	144
Departments in an office	.86	Ratings	14
Administrative-technical personnel	.12	Ratings	124
Truck drivers—	.14	Ratings	28
large work groups	−.21	Objective	
Positioners—	.18	Ratings	24
small work groups	.02	Objective	
Female sales clerks	−.03	Ratings	94
Employees in an electronics firm	.11	Ratings	377
Supervisors in an electronics firm	.13	Ratings	145
Supervisors in a package delivery company	.21	Ratings	96

Source: adapted from Vroom (1964).

performance. There is little or no correlation between the two in all but a couple of the twenty studies listed. The median correlation of .14 suggests that only about 2 percent of the variance in performance is related to satisfaction scores.

There are two viable explanations for the absence of a strong relationship of satisfaction to performance.[3] First, Vroom (1964) and Porter and Lawler (1968) argued that this "non-finding" is quite consistent with a number of theories. For example, expectancy theory suggests that performance has a direct impact on satisfaction (due to outcomes received for performance) but that any effect of satisfaction on performance is quite indirect and therefore not very strong.

The second type of explanation focuses on situational factors that may influence the relationship of satisfaction to performance. Herman (1973) has developed the idea that situational contingencies limit the strength of this relationship. She argued that workers do not have much freedom to vary performance levels because the possible range of performance is often determined by dependence on machines, on other workers, or on the worker's ability level. The acceptable range of performance is typically limited at the top by peer pressure and at the bottom by company policy. Thus, if the range of performance levels available to workers is small, satisfaction cannot have an impact on performance because the worker is not free (or able) to alter his or her output to any substantial degree.

COMMUNICATION FUNCTION

The organizational survey can serve as a communication device in two ways. First, the survey can provide a direct communication channel from workers to management. Since surveys typically guarantee anonymity to respondents, workers should feel free to communicate information that would not normally be expressed directly to management. Thus, the survey can sometimes function as a catalyst and almost always as a "safe" channel for upward communication.

3. *An excellent discussion of these explanations can be found in an article by Schwab and Cummings, 1970.*

Second, surveys can stimulate downward communication. The feedback session provides a situation in which it is socially and organizationally acceptable for management and workers to discuss issues. Numerous problems can be addressed, but more importantly, many imagined problems can be avoided. For example, a manager may learn that workers support a recent restructuring of their work but resent the manner in which it was explained. In such a case, resolution of a minor problem could salvage the effectiveness of a major organizational change.

TRAINING FUNCTION

This function is often overlooked by many organizations although it can be one of the most important products of the survey procedure. The involvement of managers in survey procedures can be an extremely enlightening experience for them and can provide both an opportunity for development of skills and for the attainment of important insights. In some organizations, managers work with survey specialists at the survey development stage to explore critical incidents in the work situation that demand further study in the survey program. By participating in the survey process, they can learn how to isolate critical incidents and how to phrase relevant questions in a language appropriate to the workers.

In other cases, survey involvement can occur at the follow-up stage. Here, managers usually work under professional guidance to help other managers interpret survey results and devise appropriate ways of reporting these results to workers. This experience can be of great value to young managers, since they are able to observe the reactions of both senior executives and employees to survey findings.

Finally, managers can participate in supervised survey teams. Managers who are trained as interviewers have the opportunity to interview workers in units other than their own. This system is a key element in many survey programs and can be a very enriching experience for most managers. It is an almost universal feeling that time spent on a survey team produces more insights into human behavior than any other developmental experience.

CORPORATE VALUE FUNCTION

Although most organizations are concerned about the welfare of their employees and often state this as an organizational objective, there is seldom any tangible and consistent measure of how well this goal is met. In some cases, it is measured indirectly and after the fact, therefore stressing negative incidents such as strikes, sabotage, or high turnover. A well-designed survey program, however, can serve as tangible evidence of an organization's concern for its employees and can provide a yardstick by which management can measure its performance. Thus, it serves as a statement of a corporate value and as a report card for guiding management behavior.

Wiggins and Steade (1976) discussed a number of issues relating to this survey function and concluded that job satisfaction is a legitimate social concern. They argued that until recently workers were willing to tolerate job dissatisfaction as long as the job was lucrative enough to allow them to enjoy off-the-job events. In other words, the quality of work life could be sacrificed for the quality of life away from work. Wiggins and Steade claim that this is changing. Because workers are no longer willing to segment their lives this way, the quality of work life is becoming central to workers.

> One's future quality of life will depend on an acceptable total-life pattern that includes increased satisfaction in the job segment.
> In this scheme, the development of people and their satisfaction in meaningful jobs will become a corporate social goal that parallels the proper utilization of other resources to meet society's needs. This will represent a corporate commitment to the humanization of work and the opportunity to grow and advance in rewarding jobs (Wiggins and Steade, 1976, p. 50).

A special task force created in 1971 by Elliot Richardson, then Secretary of Health, Education, and Welfare, to examine "...health, education and welfare problems from the perspective of one of the fundamental social institutions—work" indicates a growing interest in the quality of work life. The rather dramatic conclusion reached by this task force was presented in its report, *Work In America* (1973), as follows:

> Our analysis on work in America leads to the conclusion: Because work is central to the lives of so many Americans, either the absence of work or employment in meaningless work is creating an increasingly intolerable situation. The human costs of this state of affairs are manifested in worker alienation, alcoholism, drug addiction, and other symptoms of poor mental health. Moreover, much of our tax money is expended in an effort to compensate for problems with at least a part of their genesis in the world of work. A great part of the staggering national bill in the areas of crime and delinquency, mental and physical health, manpower and welfare are generated in our national policies and attitudes toward work (p. 86).

Or, in the words of Albert Camus, "Without work all life goes rotten. But when work is soulless, life stifles and dies."

FINANCIAL IMPACT OF EMPLOYEE ATTITUDES

Although the results of organizational surveys are usually somewhat subtle, attempts have been made recently to document these results by using hard figures. Likert (1961) applied the term *Human Resource Accounting (HRA)* to a category of methods for developing indicators of the state of organizations. While there have been a number of efforts to develop HRA systems for organizations (e.g. Alexander, 1971; Flamholtz, 1974; Herrick, 1975; Macy and Mirvis, 1976), the systems developed by Likert (1973) and Likert and Bowers (1973) can serve as an example. Their system assesses the relatively short-term costs of worker behavior. By correlating attitude scores with costs of these behaviors, it predicts changes in unit cost from changes in attitudes.

Using a variation of the HRA method, Mirvis and Lawler (1977) empirically evaluated the financial impact of job attitudes for 160 tellers at a midwestern bank. Their study—an application of Likert's ideas—measured the tellers' job satisfaction and the tellers' beliefs about which levels of performance would lead to which outcomes. They related these measurements to absenteeism, turnover, and performance (tellers' balance shortages) and evaluated them to reflect short-term costs. Their analysis indicated that an improvement in the tellers' job satisfaction of one-half of a standard deviation (a moderate increase) would lead to a predicted direct savings of $17,664 and a potential total-cost saving of $125,160 over the course of a year. This is a potential savings of $782 per teller per year.

The reader should be cautious in evaluating Human Resources Accounting techniques. These methods are fairly new and still need considerable developmental work. They do hold promise, however, for substantiating the economic value of worker attitudes. Although this approach seems to ignore the growing social concern for the quality of work life, these two positions are not mutually exclusive. It is entirely appropriate to value worker attitudes from both a social and an economic perspective. In fact, in one sense, the HRA approach does little more than quantify in financial terms a dividend that the socially concerned organization is likely to receive for improving worker attitudes.

REFERENCES

Alexander, M. Investments in people. *Canadian Chartered Accountant,* 1971, 98:1-8.

Brayfield, A. H. and Crockett, W. H. Employee attitudes and employee performance. *Psychological Bulletin,* 1955, 52: 396-424.

Dunham, R. B. Affective responses to task characteristics: The role of organizational functions. Unpublished Ph.D. dissertation, University of Illinois, 1975.

Dunham, R. B. Two job evaluation techniques and determinants of pay satisfaction. Paper presented at the convention of the American Psychological Association, Toronto, Ontario, Canada, 1978.

Dunham, R. B., Newman, J. E. and Blackburn, R. S. Employee

reactions to technological and organizational changes. Paper presented at the convention of the Midwest Psychological Association, Chicago, 1978.

Flamholtz, E. G. *Human Resource Accounting,* Dickenson, 1974.

Fleishman, E. A. and Harris, E. F. Patterns of leadership behavior related to employee grievances and turnover. *Personnel Psychology,* 1962, 15:43-56.

Fleishman, E. A., Harris, E. F., and Burtt, H. E. *Leadership and supervision in individuals.* Ohio State University, Personnel Research Board, 1955.

Getman, J. G., Goldberg, S. B., and Herman, J. B. *Union representation elections: Law and reality,* Russell Sage Foundation, 1976.

Hamner, W. C. and Smith, F. J. Work attitudes as predictors of unionization activity. *Journal of Applied Psychology,* 1978, 63:415-21.

Heneman, H. G. III and Schwab, D. P. Work and rewards theory. In *Motivation and commitment.* Bureau of National Affairs, 1975.

Herman, J. B. Are situational contingencies limiting job attitude-job performance relationships? *Organizational Behavior and Human Performance,* 1973, 10:208-24.

Herrick, N. Q. *The quality of work and its outcomes: Estimating potential increases in labor productivity.* The Academy of Contemporary Problems, 1975.

Herzberg, F., Mausner, B., Peterson, R. O., and Capwell, D. F. *Job attitudes: Review of research opinion.* Psychological Series of Pittsburgh, 1957.

Hulin, C. L. Job satisfaction and turnover in a female clerical population. *Journal of Applied Psychology,* 1966, 50:280-85.

Hulin, C. L. Effects of changes in job satisfaction levels and employee turnover. *Journal of Applied Psychology,* 1968, 52:122-26.

Likert, R. *New Patterns of Management.* McGraw-Hill, 1961.

Likert, R. Human resource accounting: Building and assessing productive organizations. *Personnel,* 1973, 50:8-24.

Likert, R. and Bowers. Improving the accuracy of P/L reports by estimating the change in dollar value of the human organization. *Michigan Business Review,* 1973, 15-24.

Macy, B. A. and Mirvis, P. H. A methodology assessment of quality of work life and organizational effectiveness in behavioral-economic terms. *Administrative Science Quarterly,* 1976, 21:212-26.

March, J. G. and Simon, H. A. *Organizations,* Wiley, 1958.

Mirvis, P. H. and Lawler, E. E. III. Measuring the financial impact of employee attitudes, *Journal of Applied Psychology,* 1977, 62:1-8.

Porter, L. W. and Lawler, E. E. III. *Managerial Attitudes and Performance,* Irwin, 1968.

Porter, L. W. and Steers, R. M. Organizational, work and personal factors in employee turnover and absenteeism, *Psychological Bulletin,* 1973, 80:151-76.

Schwab, D. P. and Cummings, L. L. Theory of performance and satisfaction: A review. *Industrial Relations,* 1970, 7: 408-30.

Smith, F. J. Problems and trends in the operational use of employee attitude measurements. Paper presented at the convention of the American Psychological Association, 1962.

Smith, F. J. Work attitudes as predictors of attendance on a specific day. *Journal of Applied Psychology,* 1977, 62: 16-19.

Vroom, V. *Work and Motivation,* Wiley, 1964.

Wiggins, R. L. and Steade, R. D. Job satisfaction as a social concern. *Academy of Management Review,* 1976, 1:48-55.

Work in America. Report of a special task force to the Secretary of Health, Education and Welfare. MIT Press, 1973.

The Survey Process: 4
How To Do It

      Survey programs are successful to the extent that they are supported at the top levels of management. It is essential, therefore, to obtain management's firm endorsement of the program. This involves more than just a simple management decision to allow a survey to be conducted. It requires a real understanding of the kind of information surveys can provide. The decision to survey should reflect management's commitment to administer the program professionally and to view the results— even if critical—in a constructive manner. With very few exceptions, managers should also agree to report the results to the respondents.

      After receiving management's support of the program, some fundamental decisions must be made. The organization must determine what to survey, when to survey, and whom to include in the survey. These considerations—the organizational analysis, the timing, and the target group, respectively—are discussed in the first section of the chapter. The last three sections explore the issues involved in developing and administering a survey program and analyze the various types of survey instruments.

PRELIMINARY CONSIDERATIONS

Organizational analysis

In establishing most personnel programs, such as the selection, training, or compensation of employees, a job analysis is a necessary first step. Similarly, in selecting or designing survey programs, an analysis of the organization and its work conditions is required. First, the organization's goals, structure, and philosophy must be examined. This information is usually gathered by interviewing executives at various levels and by studying policy statements, organizational charts, and other related documents.

Second, the factors that affect work life and organizational effectiveness should be analyzed. The following factors must be understood because they will probably be the major focus of the survey instrument: the organization's preferred or dominant leadership style and the hierarchical arrangement of supervisory positions; the reward system, both financial and nonfinancial; the sequence and flow of the work; the frequency of interpersonal contact or cooperation; the physical work environment; and the barriers to communication.

This analysis is usually accomplished by in-depth interviews with managers and employees in different parts of the organization. In some cases, job descriptions, training manuals, and other personnel information can provide valuable insights into the advantages and disadvantages of working in a given organization. Still another source of information can be provided by actual observation of on-the-job activities. Finally, analysts can actually carry out some of the duties required of the employees to supplement the analysis. In this process, in-house professionals may have a decided advantage because of their knowledge of the organization, jobs, and employee needs.

Although the procedures are similar, an organizational analysis is more extensive than a traditional job analysis because it assesses such things as personal and organizational goals, social and interpersonal interaction, supervisory and subordinate relationships, and technical and social demands of the job and organization. Without this kind of analysis, the questions included in a survey may be irrelevant in a given situation, or they may be meaningless to a particular group of employees because they are too general.

Timing of a survey

Surveys can be most effective if they are set up as part of a regularly scheduled, long-term program. This resolves the problem of scheduling particular units, departments, or locations and allows everyone involved in the survey to anticipate and plan accordingly. It also eliminates the "crisis" survey—an unscheduled survey that is carried out in response to a critical organizational problem. Rarely is the crisis approach as successful as one that has been systematically planned and scheduled.

On the other hand, in the developmental stages of a program, surveys will probably not be regularly scheduled. Experimental surveys may be tried out on a small scale and if they are successful, a broader, regularly scheduled program can be established. In these early stages of program development or in the case of single surveys, timing is also an important consideration.

The decision of when to conduct a survey usually can be resolved by good common sense. In some organizations, for example, the seasonal flow of work may create periods of increased work loads in different locations at different times. By scheduling surveys to avoid these periods, a continuing survey process can be established.

Other considerations also influence the timing of surveys. It would be unwise to schedule a survey during atypical periods such as yearly inventory or during a major production drive or sales event. It may not only be unwise but illegal to conduct a survey during an organizing campaign or during labor negotiations. It would be impractical to schedule surveys during a heavy vacation season because this might aggravate a staff shortage problem. Moreover, many people who might like to participate in a survey or who could provide valuable information might be unavailable. Thus, although surveys usually represent a welcome opportunity for employees to voice their opinions, they cause some disruption of the day-to-day operations of the company. Both impacts should be considered. However, surveys can be conducted under many conditions and at almost any time if presented and administered properly. It is this almost universal applicability that makes surveys both appealing and practical as organizational assessment techniques.

One of the advantages of the regularly scheduled organizational survey is the opportunity it gives managers of individual stores or plants to schedule both people and operations to allow for maximum participation of employees with minimal interruption of operations. In one organization, for example, surveys are scheduled on a regular basis with one third of the company's units being surveyed each year. These surveys are always scheduled well in advance of the actual survey date.

Although timing is important in survey administration, it should not be used as an excuse to avoid a survey. Reasons can always be found for *not* conducting a survey, but overreacting to any of these could lead to needless delays or even to cancellation of the survey. In fact, a typical avoidance response of managers who may be defensive about a survey in their unit is to claim that the "time is not right." While such excuses should always be given an impartial hearing by the survey administrator, they should be approached with healthy skepticism.

Target group of a survey

The group of employees to be surveyed is a basic question. Should a program include all levels of an organization or focus on only one? Should it survey a sample of employees or be a complete canvass? Should it include only regular employees or also part-time and marginally employed workers? Should a survey be limited to members of a given segment, function, or occupation within an organization, or should it cover all groups?

The answers to these kinds of questions are necessarily equivocal. No theory or proven set of rules seems to apply. However, there are a number of factors that allow survey administrators to answer these questions for a given organizational situation.

Should a survey include all levels of an organization? • The whole history of surveys in business and industry seems to be based on attempts to measure the attitudes of hourly or nonexempt employees. Only recently has any major attempt been made to survey executives' or managers' attitudes. Some of the earliest attempts to survey management were carried out at Sears by Bentz (1957) and Smith (1959).

Because of the traditional differences between management and non-management jobs and because of the differences in their corresponding responsibilities and compensation, it is unlikely that a single survey instrument could always be applied to both levels. Survey programs, however, can and have been designed to include both levels, and there is growing evidence of the value of such an approach. For example, the results of one large-scale survey of executives at Sears laid the groundwork for, and facilitated the implementation of, a new compensation program, which would otherwise have taken a much longer time to accomplish (Smith and Porter, 1977). Because executives often have a broad grasp of organizational problems and considerable control over various programs, their opinions can be valuable in making decisions at the top levels of management.

Though executives represent a unique and rich source of organizational information, they often present special logistical problems for survey administration. For example, it can be difficult to administer a survey of a small group of executives in an isolated location and preserve the anonymity of their responses. Such problems can usually be solved by making special arrangements, but they can rarely be handled by routine survey procedures.

Should employee groups be sampled or canvassed? • Several factors should be considered in this decision. The first is cost. It is much less expensive to sample (survey a representative subgroup of the target population) than to canvass (survey the entire population). A survey administrator should weigh the cost of a sample or canvass against the quality and depth of information provided by each approach.

Second, the applicability of survey questions to the members of the group being surveyed must be determined. When the questions are straightforward and have universal applicability and when detailed descriptions of small, specific groups or demographic categories are not required, sampling can produce highly accurate estimates of attitudes in a given population. In surveys of such issues as employee benefit programs, a sampling procedure can be highly effective. Because such surveys typically focus on elements of a program that are applicable to all employees and because questions dealing with such issues can be easily understood, they can be readily administered. Moreover, if surveys are designed properly, specific occupational and demographic groups can be represented and identified for appropriate analysis.

In many situations, however, even a properly designed sample survey cannot be easily conducted. The company may be very large and not have a central list of employees from which a representative sample could be randomly selected. Because of turnover or rapidly changing conditions, the survey administrator may not even know the representation of various demographic, racial, or occupational groups within the organization. In such cases, a canvass approach may be more practical and may even be less expensive. In other instances, it may be necessary to obtain exact results from specific work groups within given units. Because sampling procedures cannot provide these isolated descriptions, a complete canvass can actually be a more practical approach.

Third, the reaction of potential respondents is a subtle but very real consideration in the decision to sample or canvass. Because employees frequently welcome a survey as a means of having their say in organizational affairs, they may resent a sampling procedure that fails to include them. On the other hand, those who are asked to participate as part of a sample may feel that they have been singled out for some reason and react negatively. These factors can lead to doubts about the survey's validity and can damage management's credibility. In these situations, the added expense of a canvass might well be justified.

There are other methods of sampling that allow employees who are not included in the sample to participate in the survey. For example, it is possible to identify the survey questionnaires of the employees in a specific, representative sample before distributing the questionnaires to them. If other employees wish to participate, they can be included in the overall survey, but their responses should be scored separately from those in the selected sample.

Finally, the decision to sample or canvass may depend on how the organization wants to use a survey program. If management intends to use the survey only to gather information about members' needs or opinions, such as in a survey about personnel policies, the sample approach is recommended. If it is part of an action-oriented research program that stresses participation by members, the canvass method should be used. In fact, when a large, decentralized organization surveys relatively small units of employees in its widely dispersed stores, offices, and plants, it is often necessary to use the canvass method to obtain accurate survey results.

The purpose of sampling is to obtain information about an entire group of workers by surveying only a portion of those workers. Thus, when a decision is made to sample rather than to canvass all employees, it is essential to use a reliable procedure. Probability sampling is the only method that accurately estimates whether the data from a given sample will represent the information that could be obtained through a canvass of all workers.

The classic form of the probability method is simple random sampling. Using this approach, every worker has an equal chance of being included in the sample. A table of random numbers (or computer-generated random numbers) must be used to choose the sample. Research has shown that people tend to choose nonrandomly even when they think they are choosing randomly. Simple random sampling provides a good representation of workers and job characteristics in the sample without having to represent all of these factors intentionally. Deviations from actual random sampling, however, will bias the sample.

There are two important variations of probability sampling. The first, stratified sampling, is useful when the critical characteristics of the total group of workers suggest that a more representative sample can be made by stratifying it. The total group of workers is divided into homogenous subgroups, or strata (e.g., departments, stores, or males and females), and then a random sample for each subgroup is taken. Although this method can provide a representative sample, it depends on the survey administrator's good judgment to be successful. The second variation, cluster sampling, involves selecting complete clusters of workers (e.g., work groups or teams) at random and then surveying all workers within the clusters. This approach can simplify the administrator's work because it reduces the number of units that must be surveyed. However, if important worker or job characteristics are not distributed evenly from cluster to cluster, the sample will probably be biased. Thus, the judgment of the survey administrator is again critical.

There are a number of methods to determine how many workers (or clusters) need to be included in a representative sample. Krejcie and Morgan (1970) provided a table to estimate the number of workers that should be included in a representative sample of all workers (see Table 4.1). This table can also be used to estimate the number of workers needed for a representative sample of various subgroups (to compare survey data of males and females, for example).

TABLE 4.1   Table for Determining Sample Size from a Given Population.

N	S	N	S	N	S
10	10	220	140	1200	291
15	14	230	144	1300	297
20	19	240	148	1400	302
25	24	250	152	1500	306
30	28	260	155	1600	310
35	32	270	159	1700	313
40	36	280	162	1800	317
45	40	290	165	1900	320
50	44	300	169	2000	322
55	48	320	175	2200	327
60	52	340	181	2400	331
65	56	360	186	2600	335
70	59	380	191	2800	338
75	63	400	196	3000	341
80	66	420	201	3500	346
85	70	440	205	4000	351
90	73	460	210	4500	354
95	76	480	214	5000	357
100	80	500	217	6000	361
110	86	550	226	7000	364
120	92	600	234	8000	367
130	97	650	242	9000	368
140	103	700	248	10000	370
150	108	750	260	15000	375
160	113	800	265	20000	377
170	118	850	269	30000	379
180	123	900	274	40000	380
190	127	950	278	50000	381
200	132	1000	285	75000	382
210	136	1100		1000000	384

Source: Krejcie and Morgan (1970).
Note: N is for any *complete* group (population). S is sample size.

Should surveys include part-time or marginally employed workers? • A significant trend in industry today is the increased use of large numbers of seasonal and part-time employees. The decision to include or to exclude these workers from surveys can involve some rather complicated considerations. Part-time employees frequently work full-time in other jobs. They may be students who seek only temporary employment or housewives or "househusbands" who will accept only particular part-time work schedules. In any case, the motivation, needs, and aspirations that part-time workers bring to their jobs can be quite different from those that regular employees have.

A number of other factors can also influence this decision. The social relations between full- and part-time employees can be a source of either conflict or interpersonal strength in a unit; the benefit and compensation programs for these two groups may or may not differ; and the legal and labor relations status of each group may be identical or vary greatly. Finally, the part-time group may be truly transient and may make only a marginal contribution to the organization, or it may represent a permanent group whose work is of key importance.

Many companies have decided to include part-time employees in organizational surveys. This decision reflects the growing importance of part-time employees in many organizations and their influence on the national economy. In many organizations, part-time and full-time employees are surveyed with the same instrument. Separate reports are prepared for each group, however, because their needs and motivations often differ. On the other hand, the inclusion of large numbers of part-time employees can often create scheduling problems for survey administration and can complicate survey implementation.

DEVELOPMENTAL STEPS

This section examines the choices that must be made during the developmental stage of the survey process. The organization must decide what type of questionnaire, professional assistance, and statistical norms to use. In addition, it must determine whether to adopt a general or in-depth approach to survey questions, whether to phrase questions at advanced or elementary reading levels, and whether to write them in English or in another language.

At this stage of the process, the organization should also decide whether the survey program will be permanent or temporary since this determination will influence each of the decisions outlined above. Because many surveys that begin on a trial basis evolve into permanent programs, administrators should look ahead even when they are planning what they think will only be a "one time survey."

Types of instruments

For a small organization or for one that is planning a single survey, the time and effort needed to develop a completely unique instrument (data-gathering device) may not always be justified. In such cases, an organization may find a standard or packaged survey suitable to its needs and may even incorporate it or a variation of it at a later time as part of a regular in-house survey program. Use of an appropriate standardized instrument can often have other advantages. For example, a number of these instruments have been carefully developed over a period of years to accurately measure specific attitudes. They are often better and much less expensive than questionnaires developed by an organization. (A section later in the chapter describes some of the available instruments.)

On the other hand, an organization should seriously consider developing its own program if it has special needs that standard survey packages cannot address. This is often the case in large, diversified, specialized, or highly complex organizations. It may also be appropriate in an organization that wishes to make the survey and its attendant feedback and followup procedures a permanent part of its personnel or employee relations program. (The steps involved in developing such a program are also discussed later in the chapter.)

Types of professional assistance

While much of survey preparation, administration, and analysis is simple and straightforward, a number of complex issues are also involved. Certain psychometric criteria should be met and some important ethical standards must be observed in any sound program. As a result, professional direction of such programs is essential: managers must decide whether to use in-house professionals or outside consultants.

Except for organizations that regularly employ professionals to administer their survey programs, most companies and institutions rely on consultants exclusively, at least in the early stages of development and often in the later stages as well. Organizations may also need outside help in constructing and administering occasional surveys that are not part of a regular system.

There are some obvious cost considerations in such decisions. If a program is to be used infrequently, the cost of hiring an in-house professional would probably not be justified unless that person could serve other functions as well. At the same time, an in-house professional may be more knowledgeable about the organization than a consultant. Because of an in-house professional's availability, he or she may also be more effective than a consultant in carrying out the followup programs that are normally a crucial part of a survey program.

Types of analyses and comparisons

Because attitude scales, like almost all psychological measures, provide only relative scores—ones that can be interpreted most effectively through comparisons with other scores—the availability of comparison scores, or norms, is very important. Norms provide average scores for various groups of workers in various types of jobs. Thus, it is possible to determine whether a sample of workers compares favorably or unfavorably to a similar referent group.

The proper interpretation of any response involves a comparison with the responses of other groups (inside and/or outside of the organization) to the same item. If a permanent program is established, the accumulation of survey results over a period of time will allow the development of norms within the organization that can be used as a basis for comparison. The occasional or one-time survey, however, will have to use norms based primarily on data from other organizations. The need for these external comparison standards leads many companies to use standard survey packages.

The most frequent mistake that managers make is to interpret a relative score in absolute terms, that is, without reference to some comparative standard. For example, managers

might react to a survey item for which 80 percent of the participants had favorable responses with such comments as, "80 percent was passing when I went to school." In reality, however, an
80 percent response by itself means little, and in comparative
terms, it may even reflect a serious problem.

It is important that a survey program provide norms that
are appropriate for the groups being surveyed. While most standard survey programs do provide such norms, the survey administrator should make certain that they are applicable to the
organization in question. The use of blue collar norms, for example, would be inappropriate for a totally white collar sample.
(Even without norms, however, it is usually possible to make
relative comparisons within a given plant or local unit based on a
single survey. This process is discussed in a later section dealing
with survey interpretation.)

Focus of survey approach

Another point to consider in the development of a survey
is its focus or direction. Undoubtedly, the most common type of
survey deals with several facets of job satisfaction, such as supervision, pay, working conditions, job pressure, and organizational
commitment. This approach can effectively assess the relative
level of job satisfaction or organizational well-being. Because it
covers many issues, however, this type of survey rarely deals
with any single issue in great depth.

Another approach, often used as an adjunct to an established program, explores one problem area thoroughly. This can
include gathering suggestions for solving the problem or
measuring anticipated reactions to proposed solutions. Although
it is less common than the other approach, it can yield some
helpful organizational results. For example, Sears used this approach to determine the reactions of service employees to a proposed change in their work schedule from five eight-hour days to
four ten-hour days. The survey concentrated on all the positive
and negative consequences of this change, including such things
as its effect on work performance, on social and leisure-time activities, and on family relationships. Using employees' reactions
and suggestions as a guide, Sears instituted the change for the
group of employees in the sample. Moreover, by following up on

the actual change in work schedules with another concentrated survey, it was possible to test employees' initial judgments and reactions and to make further refinements that have helped to maintain the successful operation of the new schedule.

Thus, the survey administrator should decide at the outset whether a broad or in-depth approach is to be taken, since this decision will influence many of the steps that follow. Frequently, it will be advantageous for a survey to have a broad scope in general but an in-depth focus on particular issues of major concern.

Language requirements

Many organizations today are multinational; they employ people of many different language backgrounds or preferences. Sometimes, survey instruments must be translated into other languages to be applicable to all employees. This is often no simple task. A translated version must be retranslated by an independent agent to insure the integrity of the original survey instrument. While often involving several such translations and retranslations, this process can be accomplished in a relatively straightforward manner. Any modified instrument, however, must be standardized as though it were a completely new instrument.

Because translated versions of a survey are usually administered in countries where only one language is spoken, they can be used without great difficulty. It is usually necessary, however, to develop norms for each country or culture, since it is unlikely that the norms developed for the original version would be appropriate. A much more severe problem occurs when two or more languages are spoken in the same organization and when results must be combined for total assessment purposes. Since many cities in the United States, Canada, and Europe are bilingual, this problem is becoming increasingly important for corporations located in those cities. It appears possible to develop two parallel language forms that will give comparable results in either language, but the translation effort is quite demanding. For example, in an elaborate study of this problem (Katterberg, Smith, and Hoy, 1977), statistically equivalent versions of a group of survey items were produced in English and Spanish.

Thus, in cities such as Miami, New York, Los Angeles, and Chicago, where large groups of both Spanish-speaking and English-speaking employees work in the same organization, it is now possible to survey both groups in their preferred language and to combine the total results for analysis.

Language preference is also an important factor in truly bilingual groups. In some countries or cultures two languages are spoken but only one is preferred or allowed. In Flemish Belgium, for instance, it was once technically illegal for an employee to be addressed in French by a manager, although most employees speak and understand both Flemish and French. Failure to observe this custom in a questionnaire might have been insulting to the respondents. In Puerto Rico, English questionnaires are often preferred over Spanish, even though Spanish is used in conversation, because much of written Spanish is too formal to use in questionnaires and because much of the education the people receive is in English.

A final consideration is the level of language used in a survey. In some instances, nonverbal techniques may be used when the level of literacy is extremely low. This seems to be a growing problem. In fact, several standard questionnaires have a sixth-grade reading level. This reading level, however, cannot always be used to assess the subtleties of many work situations; the instrument often has to be supplemented by interviews. Nor can this level of language be used effectively among employees with higher language levels. In such cases, questions with a more demanding reading level must also be included.

Once the organizational analysis is completed and the language level ascertained, the survey administrator is usually able to decide whether to use a standard survey instrument or to develop a special instrument to fit the organization's needs.

TYPES OF SURVEYS

Because questionnaires are the most frequently used survey instruments, this section concentrates on the steps involved in selecting standard versions and in developing questionnaires tailored to a given organization or situation. (Even if interviews are used, the developmental questions outlined in the preceding section are equally relevant. Appendix I contains a guide to a nondirective interview process intended to be used in conjunction with a questionnaire survey program.)

Choice of standard survey instruments

More than one hundred instruments have been used to measure job satisfaction. Most of these instruments, unfortunately, are deficient for one reason or another. On the other hand, several job satisfaction instruments with desirable psychometric qualities have been developed. This section discusses four well-known questionnaires—the Job Descriptive Index, the Minnesota Satisfaction Questionnaire, the Index of Organizational Reactions, and the Faces Scale—that have been used successfully in a wide variety of organizations (see Appendix III for validation study). Under many circumstances, the use of one of these instruments can be successful for forming the core of a survey.[1]

The following issues, which are included in our discussion of the four job satisfaction questionnaires, should be considered when choosing a standard survey instrument:

1) reliability
2) validity
3) content and scale type
4) administration time
5) language level
6) norm availability
7) facets of satisfaction measured

The terms *reliability* and *validity* must be understood in order to evaluate survey instruments. *Reliability* is the ability of an instrument to measure with a relative absence of error. If an instrument is reliable, it will tend to produce the same results for different survey administrators. The more precise a satisfaction instrument is, the more reliable it is likely to be. Synonyms of reliability include dependability, stability, consistency, and ac-

---

1. *Other successful questionnaires have been developed, but they are usually available only through the services of professional consulting or survey organizations. Two of these instruments are discussed in some detail by Miller (1969).*

curacy. Reliability is increased by 1) using unambiguous questions, 2) including several items to measure a particular attitude (to prevent inaccurate interpretations of one question), 3) providing clear instructions, and 4) standardizing survey administration conditions.

Validity is the ability of an instrument to measure what it is intended to measure. For example, if answers to a job satisfaction questionnaire are influenced by anything other than actual job satisfaction, its validity is reduced. The validity of an instrument can be explored 1) by examining the content of questions for appropriateness; 2) by examining relationships of the scores to behaviors which should be influenced by (or influence) those being measured; or 3) by comparing it to other measures intended to assess the same factor. In general, scores from one factor (e.g., pay satisfaction) should converge with other measures of the same factor more than with measures of other factors (e.g., work satisfaction or co-worker satisfaction).

Studies have shown that all four instruments discussed here are reliable and valid (see Appendix III). Poor administration procedures, however, can lead to unsatisfactory results even with these instruments because the effectiveness of a very good tool depends upon the user's skill. Tables 4.2–4.5 present examples of the four instruments.

The Job Descriptive Index (JDI), developed by Smith, Kendall, and Hulin (1969), is one of the most widely used job satisfaction instruments. With seventy-two items in what is called a modified adjective checklist format, the JDI measures satisfaction with pay, promotion, co-workers, supervision, and the quality of work. The JDI is especially appropriate for employees with relatively low levels of literacy and requires only

TABLE 4.2   Job Descriptive Index: Sample Items.

Directions:	Think of your present work. What is it like most of the time?		
	Circle YES if it describes your work.		
	Circle NO if it does NOT describe it.		
	Circle ? if you cannot decide.		
Fascinating	YES	NO	?
Routine	YES	NO	?
Satisfying	YES	NO	?

Source: Smith, Kendall, and Hulin (1969).

TABLE 4.3   Minnesota Satisfaction Questionnaire: Sample Items.

The purpose of this section is to give you a chance to tell how you feel about your present job, what things you are satisfied with and what things you are dissatisfied with. Listed below are statements about your present job. Decide how satisfied you feel about the aspect of your job described by the statement. After each statement indicate the number which best describes your feelings. Use the following scales to indicate your judgments:

1	2	3	4	5
Not Satisfied	Slightly Satisfied	Satisfied	Very Satisfied	Extremely Satisfied

ON MY PRESENT JOB, THIS IS HOW I FEEL ABOUT . . .

The chance to be of service to others	1	2	3	4	5
The chance to try out some of my own ideas	1	2	3	4	5
Being able to do the job without feeling it is morally wrong	1	2	3	4	5
The chance to work by myself	1	2	3	4	5
The variety in my work	1	2	3	4	5

Source: Weiss, Dawis, England, and Lofquist (1967).

TABLE 4.4   Index of Organizational Reactions: Sample Items.

The people who supervise me have:
1. many more good traits than bad ones
2. more good traits than bad ones
3. about the same number of good traits as bad ones
4. more bad traits than good ones
5. many more bad traits than good ones

The supervision I receive is the kind that:
1. greatly discourages me from giving extra effort
2. tends to discourage me from giving extra effort
3. has little influence on me
4. encourages me to give extra effort
5. greatly encourages me to give extra effort

How does the way you are treated by those who supervise you influence your *overall attitude* toward your job?

1. It has a very unfavorable influence.
2. It has a slightly unfavorable influence.
3. It has no real effect.
4. It has a favorable influence.
5. It has a very favorable influence.

Source: Smith (1976).

TABLE 4.5   Faces Scales: Sample Items.

Consider the work itself and the things you actually do on your job. Circle the face on the appropriate scale which best expresses how you feel about the *work itself*.

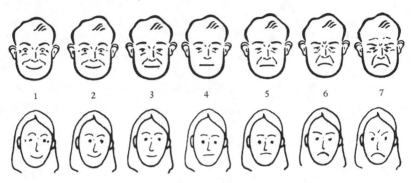

Source: Kunin (1955); Dunham and Herman (1975).

ten to fifteen minutes to administer. The extensive normative information available is somewhat dated, however; it has not been revised since the questionnaire was developed. A large body of validity and reliability evidence for the JDI suggests good psychometric properties. A Spanish version of the JDI is available and has received initial support for reliability and validity (Katterberg, Smith, and Hoy, 1977).

The Minnesota Satisfaction Questionnaire (MSQ), developed by Weiss, Dawis, England, and Lofquist (1967), consists of a set of one hundred evaluative items that measure satisfaction with the following facets:

1) Ability utilization
2) Achievement
3) Activity
4) Advancement
5) Authority
6) Company policies and practices
7) Compensation
8) Co-workers
9) Creativity
10) Independence
11) Moral values
12) Recognition
13) Responsibility
14) Security
15) Social service
16) Social status
17) Supervision— human relations
18) Supervision— technical
19) Variety
20) Working conditions

Although a number of these facets have been well validated (see
Appendix III) and all are apparently reliable, some of the dimensions have received relatively little study. Our analyses of the
MSQ suggested that most, but not all of the twenty dimensions
have reasonably good validity evidence. The MSQ requires a
moderate level of literacy and takes from twenty to forty minutes
to administer. (A shortened version requiring only five to ten
minutes to administer is available, but it does not appear to
adequately assess all twenty dimensions.) Some normative data is
also available for the MSQ.

The Index of Organizational Reactions (IOR), developed
by Sears, Roebuck, and Company (see Smith, 1976; Dunham,
Smith, and Blackburn, 1977), utilizes forty-two items to assess
eight satisfaction facets: pay, promotion, co-workers, supervision, the quality of the work, the amount of work, the physical
conditions of the work surroundings, and company identification
(policies and practices). The IOR requires a moderate level of
language skills and takes from ten to fifteen minutes to administer. There is very good validity and reliability evidence for the
IOR (see Appendix III) but this data, as well as normative information, is based primarily on Sears, Roebuck and Company and
its employees. Sears has surveyed over a million people since
1962 with the IOR. A Spanish version of the IOR was developed
and validated in the same study in which the Spanish version of
the JDI was studied (Katterberg, Smith, and Hoy, 1977).

The Faces Scales, developed by Kunin (1955) and by
Dunham and Herman (1975), consist of a set of male and female
faces with matching expressions. The scales were originally designed to assess general satisfaction levels. Recently, however, it
has been shown that the scales may be used to validly assess at
least eight facets of satisfaction by carefully changing the worded
instructions that accompany the faces (see Appendix III). Administration of the Faces Scales requires very little time, and
only very low language skills are needed to understand it. Since
the characteristics of the response scale have been validated for
use with any satisfaction facet, great flexibility is possible. Reliability evidence, while limited, is supportive of the stability of
the scales. The Faces Scales can effectively assess workers' overall responses to particular facets. It is often used as the conclud-
ing instrument of a survey or in an exploratory area. It is usually
well received by employees. No normative data are currently
available, however.

Development of special questionnaires

In designing a questionnaire for use in a particular organizational setting, any of the item formats of the four questionnaires presented in the preceding section could be used. The goal is to design questions that will elicit employee reactions to the specific conditions that the organizational analysis identifies as important.

Wording and format of questions • While the writing of items is an art and requires sensitivity as well as skill, the process does have certain well-recognized rules which should be observed. Whole books are devoted to this subject, and the reader is advised to consult one or more of them (Oppenheim, 1966; Leman, 1973, Shaw and Wright, 1967). Suffice it to say that the art of item writing is not nearly as easy as it appears.

The content of items depends upon how the questionnaire will be used. Specific questions may apply to one group of employees but not to another. For example, a series of items designed to measure the detailed responses of employees in clerical and office jobs will be of little use in measuring reactions to blue-collar jobs. On the other hand, extremely general items will not be useful in describing the nuances of particular job situations.

Organizations with large, established survey programs have solved this dilemma by devising several questionnaires and dividing each into two parts: 1) a core of generally worded items that apply in almost all situations; and 2) a supplemental group of specific items that are tailored to given jobs or settings. All questionnaires include the core items while the supplemental items used in any particular questionnaire version depend on their relevance to the work or job setting being studied. With this combination of core and supplemental items, it is possible to design a series of survey instruments that provides both the basic index of job satisfaction needed for comparing one group to another and the detailed aspects of each job or organizational setting.

In this hybrid approach to survey design, the items that make up the core are often constructed in an evaluative mode—one that reflects an overall favorable or unfavorable reaction to a given category such as pay, supervision, or co-workers. The following question is an example of an evaluative item.

Q: How do you feel about your physical working conditions?

1) Extremely satisfied
2) Well satisfied
3) Only moderately satisfied
4) Somewhat dissatisfied
5) Very dissatisfied

Because such items are used for measuring job satisfaction for a wide range of situations, they are usually grouped into scales or categories and thus should meet certain psychometric requirements. For example, it is important that the items measuring reactions to one category not overlap in meaning or content with those used in another category. Some type of statistical technique, such as factor analysis, is usually used to determine the degree of independence among items or scales in a questionnaire (see Appendix III).

The supplemental items are frequently written in a descriptive mode—one that calls for respondents to simply acknowledge that a given condition does or does not exist, rather than making an evaluation of it. For example, an item which asks: "Does your supervisor conduct performance reviews each year?" calls for a simple "yes" or "no" response and should be answerable regardless of how the employee feels about the supervisor or the performance review. Unfortunately, evaluative and descriptive items are often not as independent as one might hope. Employees who dislike their supervisor are more likely to deny that he or she conducts performance reviews than employees who like their supervisors. In spite of this admitted overlap, the distinction is worthwhile. The responses made to a set of descriptive items can provide insights into the reasons for a high or low level of job satisfaction in a given group. Thus, a crude cause-and-effect analysis of organizational conditions and employee reactions to them is made possible by including both descriptive and evaluative items.

Because descriptive items can often be used only in the setting being studied, they frequently do not form scales but are treated as single, discrete measures. However, reliable items that have no overlap in content with other items are also important here. Again, items are usually selected on the basis of purity and clarity of content, reliability, and relevance to specific situations.

In a continuing survey program, descriptive items can be selected from a large pool of questions whose usefulness and reliability has been established through repeated uses. Relevant items that provide a balanced distribution of responses, that correlate moderately with other related items, and that yield reliable responses from participants in different target groups are the most useful supplemental items in any questionnaire.

Pilot test of items • Unless an organization has had success with a given item or item pool, it is important to conduct some type of pilot study before actually using a questionnaire. Among other things, a proper pilot study should aim at eliminating items that produce ambiguous responses or highly skewed distributions of responses. In many cases this can be determined by simple inspection.

Frequently, the ambiguity of items and the reactions of respondents can also be determined by having a pilot study group actually "talk through" a questionnaire. With this approach, a preliminary draft of each survey questionnaire can be administered to a sample of employees who are representative of the eventual target group. After completing this preliminary survey, an entire day can be devoted to group discussion of the individual items. Employees are asked to verbalize their interpretations of, and responses to each item. This process can identify and correct many serious blunders in item writing or construction before the final questionnaire is administered. For example, one group of employees with a particular ethnic background interpreted the item "My boss frequently passes the buck" to mean that the supervisor paid employees well.

Group discussion is also likely to reveal specific incidents or conditions that cause employees to respond in a particular way to a given item. Because the company has many similar units, these specific conditions are likely to be found in numerous locations. The identification of these conditions can help survey administrators to interpret survey results for local managers and to make many specific suggestions for followup action. For example, an item that included the statement "Some of the things I am required to do on my job are physically too much for me" was found to refer to a specific task in one particular job. But because the same task and the same job were found to occur in many similar units, they became the focus of corrective action.

Placement of items in questionnaire • Another specific concern in designing a questionnaire is the actual placement of items within it. After items have been assigned to categories, they must either be grouped together by categories or placed randomly in the questionnaire. In some cases, items are assigned at random in order to break up any response set or predisposition on the part of the respondent. In other cases, items are grouped to bring out this tendency. As far as statistical results are concerned, either arrangement seems appropriate. A pioneering study of this problem (Baer, 1953) found that either type of placement resulted in nearly identical profiles of item results.

Other considerations, however, seem to argue in favor of grouping related items in a questionnaire. Respondents often complain that the same item was repeated throughout a questionnaire when, in fact, no such duplication actually occurred. What probably did occur is that one item in a category that appeared early in the questionnaire seemed similar to another item in the same category that appeared later. For example, these two items may appear in different places in the same questionnaire: (1) "Pay is handled poorly around here" and (2) "My pay is poor for the work I do." While these items actually address different aspects of the same category (compensation), they are frequently perceived as identical when widely separated in a questionnaire. This perceived redundancy frequently leads respondents to suspect that the questionnaire was designed to trick them and this, in turn, can defeat the whole purpose of the survey instrument. Thus, by grouping together all items of the same category, the respondent can see the actual variation in the content and purpose of items. Grouping also allows the respondent to see the differences between categories of items and tends to discourage a generalized response to all areas.

SURVEY ADMINISTRATION PROCEDURES

The administration of survey instruments to respondents is a fundamental step in the survey process. Unless this is done properly, much of the developmental work and subsequent analysis of data can be rendered useless. The goal here is to establish *standardized conditions* under which survey instruments are administered so that administrative procedures do not influence survey results.

Deciding on a survey administrator

In some organizations, consultants or other outside experts administer the instrument; in others, in-house professionals are responsible for survey administration. Even line personnel can administer surveys if their training is adequate and if step-by-step procedures are clearly defined. Undoubtedly, the use of professionals or para-professionals is the best procedure to follow. In such instances, errors and problems will be kept to a minimum by observance of established techniques of survey and test administration.

The size or structure of many organizations, however, may preclude the use of professional help. The respondents of surveys in large or decentralized organizations may work in widely scattered locations. Although the need for frequent surveys may be greatest in these organizations, the use of professional survey administrators is often too costly and impractical. A common solution to such a problem is to have managers at different locations administer the survey instruments according to specific guidelines established by professionals. If properly monitored for compliance and data quality, these instruments can yield information that is comparable to the data collected by professionals. This is not accomplished easily or automatically, however. It may be necessary to test and retest the procedures in realistic settings. At Sears, for example, a series of studies was conducted in which different sets of administrative instructions were tried with field personnel as administrators. After several trials, a set of detailed and carefully written instructions emerged. They were presented to half of the employees by their unit managers and to the other half by outside professionals. The results, which were compiled from tests at several locations, clearly indicated that no statistically significant or practical differences existed.

It should be pointed out, however, that during the preliminary studies different results were obtained when managers or other nonprofessionals were allowed to deviate from a standard approach. Such things as funny asides, off-hand jokes, or other ad-libbed comments seemed to create an atmosphere that affected results. At one meeting, for example, a manager made a joking reference to the large number of people who had applied for work at the store in the past month. Later, it was shown that the results of that meeting were much more negative than the results of twelve other meetings that he conducted in a standard fashion. Thus, the success of any survey administration procedure at the local level by the local manager depends on the care with which instructions are written and the rigor with which they are observed.

Although local or line managers are more likely to make errors when administering surveys than professionals are, there are some advantages to such an approach. One of these is the local manager's increased feeling of "owning the program." By administering the survey, managers are better able to present them as programs that they endorse and sponsor. When people from outside a unit are used, local managers often view this as an intrusion and may feel some loss of managerial prerogative. Since managers are often responsible for everything that happens in a unit, having the manager administer the program may strongly contribute to its success. Moreover, managers in many organizations are quite comfortable administering surveys since the procedure is very similar to many other data-gathering programs that they are required to handle. As a result, their participation, if properly guided, is not nearly as error-prone as it may first appear.

Presenting the survey

The following procedure is one which we have found to be successful. With appropriate modifications, it can be applied in both large and small organizations.

Scheduling of survey meetings • Surveys are scheduled a year in advance, and managers are given the exact date for their survey approximately six weeks ahead of time. At this time, the questionnaires and accompanying materials are sent to the manager. In large stores or plants, it may be necessary to conduct many meetings in order to give all employees a chance to participate, while in small organizations one or two meetings may be sufficient. Meetings are scheduled during work hours and all questionnaires are completed at the meetings. If this creates a fairly difficult scheduling problem, survey administration often extends over an entire week.

Number of employees at each meeting • Although all employees are scheduled to be included in the survey program, participation is completely voluntary. When the program is well accepted, over 90 percent of the employees in any given unit will probably choose to take part. Although attendance at meetings may vary, an attempt is made to include a minimum of twenty-five employees whenever possible. This not only helps to reduce the number of meetings, but more importantly, it helps encourage a feeling of anonymity that might be lost in a smaller meeting. It should be noted, however, that it is usually difficult for one administrator to handle more than fifty persons at once.

Preparation of questionnaires and instructions • A unit or department manager may be responsible for conducting these meetings. Questionnaires should either be placed on seats of chairs before employees enter the room or picked up randomly by employees as they enter. Seating arrangements are determined by employees themselves in order to alleviate employee concerns about secretly coded questionnaires.

A real attempt should be made to create a relaxed climate. This is partly accomplished by devoting the entire meeting to the survey—no other business or subject should be presented or discussed. Once the people are seated, the administrator should introduce the subject and indicate that because it is necessary to present the program in a standard manner, it is essential to read the instructions. He or she then proceeds with the instructions, pausing at predetermined points to ask for questions or to assure respondents' understanding. (A modified set of standard instructions is included in Appendix II.)

A list of suggested cautions regarding what to do and what not to do in conducting the meeting is also included as part of the survey instructions to the administrator. Some of these depend on common sense but most come from our experience with such meetings. The administrator also receives suggestions on how to answer frequent or typical questions that may arise. These, of course, will vary from one organization to another, but the survey administrator should be aware that such questions do occur repeatedly and that a system should be devised for handling them. The following examples suggest how to handle three frequently asked questions.

"Why are we doing a survey now?" Here, the administrator can usually respond by merely referring to company policy. For example: "The survey program is scheduled to cover one third of all units each year. At the beginning of each year, units are scheduled for the whole year." The manager may then remind employees that the last survey in this particular unit was about three years ago.

"Will we see the results?" This is a good opportunity to spell out the steps in a survey. The administrator can indicate that once the report of the overall findings has been received, meetings will be scheduled to share the results with employees.

"Why were we selected to take the survey?" In organizations where a sampling approach is used, this question may be common. The best response is simply to explain whatever procedure is being used. Most employees know about opinion polls and accept sampling procedures. In companies that encourage all employees to participate, the question is rarely asked.

Another question that is less frequently posed has to do with the authorship of the questionnaire. It can range from the abusive—"What genius wrote this?"—to the complimentary— "This hits the nail on the head. Who put this together?" Again, if it is necessary to answer at all, the manager should make the authorship clear.

While this overall administrative procedure appears to be rigid, in practice it works quite smoothly. Most administrators who have had several experiences with the program find it fairly easy to follow and straightforward in its application. At the same time, administrators should not deviate from the standard procedures. Penalties should be attached to any serious deviation.

Monitoring the meeting • Administrators should be instructed to present the survey instructions to their employees and to answer all employees' questions. If, for whatever reason, the administrator's presence seems threatening to the employees, it is often best for the individual to leave the room at this point. For most meetings, however, monitors may need to be appointed if the administrator leaves. In such cases, members of the unit's staff are used, but they are instructed to remain at the front of the room and to respond only when asked a question. Monitors should not circulate or create the impression that they are watching employees. When a consultant serves as administrator, problematic threats are not as likely to be perceived. Although this kind of rigidity and discipline may be totally unimportant to a vast majority of respondents, it is absolutely essential for those who do feel some concern or apprehension about their responses.

Collection and treatment of questionnaires • One informal but highly successful procedure for handling completed questionnaires consists of utilizing employee mailing committees. In their final instructions, administrators indicate that all completed questionnaires are to be placed in a large box located near the exit. At this time, the administrator appoints two employees in the meeting to serve as a mailing committee. They are given packing material and a preaddressed mailing label to the scoring facility and are responsible for actually placing the packet of completed questionnaires in an outside mail box. Variations of this method can be used, but the primary purpose is to assure anonymity of responses.

Since all questionnaires for a given meeting are immediately sent to the scoring facility, employees are reassured that their questionnaires will not be seen by local management at any time. This particular phase of the procedure seems to be well accepted by employees. It also expedites handling of survey results and eliminates any chance of questionnaires being lost or misplaced within the unit.

There are other ways of handling completed forms. When surveys are administered by consultants, they often collect the questionnaires. In other cases, addressed and stamped envelopes can be provided to respondents for individual mailing. This procedure is workable but does result in some loss of surveys. Apparently, some people forget or for other reasons, fail to mail their questionnaires.

Another variation of this approach is to have the questionnaires addressed to an independent agency where they are removed from their envelopes. Well-known auditing or consulting firms are usually equipped to handle this type of program. This particular procedure is helpful if there is some need or desire to assure respondents that their "postal mark" will not be used to identify them or their specific location.

Monitoring the administrative procedures

Even if instructions are explicit and carefully followed, there are always a number of things that can and will go wrong, especially when inexperienced people administer the instruments. It is best, therefore, to set up systems for monitoring survey administration so that any serious problem can be discovered and its recurrence prevented.

One form of monitoring is to have experienced survey administrators sit in on survey sessions. This is frequently done and is effective as long as their presence does not disturb the group or the person administering the survey. In many organizations, the presence of an outsider could be very disruptive. In such a case, other approaches should be considered. For example, the questionnaires themselves can be used to provide information about the adequacy of administrative practices. A question or two might be included to get at the perceived fairness of the administration. In many instances, a high percentage of negative responses will point to problems created by a particular administrator or by a unique situation.

Employee comments are also a fruitful source of monitoring information. In some cases, employees may use portions of the questionnaire to evaluate the instructions or the presentation of the survey and to suggest improvements. In other instances, the sheer volume of employee comments will be an indication of the adequacy or inadequacy of survey administration. For example, about 40 percent of the employees at Sears can be expected to write in comments of one kind or another. Whenever the response rate for a given store or unit goes well below 40 percent, there is a good chance the survey was not administered properly. This is usually confirmed in subsequent interviews with the employees. In some cases, instructions were not followed properly, employees were encouraged to hurry their responses, or some other extraneous influence was present.

REFERENCES

Baer, M. E. A simplified procedure for the measurement of employee attitudes. *Journal of Applied Psychology,* 1953, 37:163-67.

Bentz, V. J. *Dimensions of executive morale.* Unpublished report. Sears, Roebuck and Co., 1957.

Dunham, R. B. and Herman, J. B. Development of a female faces scale for measuring job satisfaction. *Journal of Applied Psychology,* 1975, 60:629-31.

Dunham, R. B., Smith, F. J., and Blackburn, R. S. Validation of the Index of Organizational Reactions (IOR) with the JDI, MSQ and Faces Scales. *Academy of Management Journal,* 1977, 20:420-32.

Katterberg, R., Smith, F. J., and Hoy, S. Language, time and person effects on attitude scale translations. *Journal of Applied Psychology,* 1977, 62:385-91.

Krejcie, R. V. and Morgan, D. W. Determining sample size for research activities. *Educational and Psychological Measurement,* 1970, 30:607-10.

Kunin, T. The construction of a new type of attitude measure. *Personnel Psychology,* 1955, 8:65-78.

Leman, N. *Attitudes and Their Measurement.* Halsted Press, 1973.

Miller, D. C. *Handbook of Research Design and Social Measurement.* McKay, 1969.

Oppenheim, A. N. *Questionnaire Design and Attitude Measurement.* Basic Books, 1966.

Shaw, M. E. and Wright, J. M. *Scales for the Measurement of Attitudes.* McGraw-Hill, 1967.

Smith, F. J. An investigation of the dimensions of executive morale. Paper presented at the convention of the American Psychological Association, 1959.

Smith, F. J. The Index of Organizational Reactions (IOR). *JSAS Catalog of Selected Documents in Psychology,* 1976, 6:Ms. No. 1265.

Smith, F. J. and Porter, L. W. What do executives really think about their organizations? *Organizational Dynamics,* Autumn 1977, 68-80.

Smith, P. C., Kendall, L. M., and Hulin, C. L. *The Measurement of Satisfaction in Work and Retirement.* Rand McNally, 1969.

Weiss, D. J., Dawis, R. V., England, G. W., and Lofquist, L. H. *Manual for the Minnesota Satisfaction Questionnaire,* Minnesota Studies in Vocational Rehabilitation: XXII, University of Minnesota Industrial Relations Center, Work Adjustment Project, 1967.

The Use of Survey Results

Once the results of a survey have been gathered, data processing can begin. The sequence involved in processing survey data is scoring, editing, analyzing, interpreting, reporting to management, and feeding back results to survey participants. These procedures should be designed and established long before the data are collected. In this way, much confusion, delay, and inefficiency can be avoided.

In the actual design of the process, however, it is often wise to approach the sequence in reverse order. That is, the final steps—the report to management and the feedback to participants—should be considered first. After these procedures have been established, the steps required in analyzing, interpreting, scoring, and editing the data can be decided. Because these procedures are more complicated in large or broadly based surveys, this discussion focuses on such approaches. If the process is appropriately modified, however, it can be applied to any survey.

SCORING AND EDITING

Before any manipulation of survey data can occur, it is necessary to establish a scoring format and an editing policy. Items are scored by assigning numbers to each item's response categories. All standard questionnaires have predetermined scoring procedures. For special questionnaires, the particular approach to attitude scaling used in the design of the questionnaire usually dictates the scoring procedure (see Edwards, 1957). After a scoring arrangement is established, it is a relatively simple matter to have the questionnaire processed by hand-scoring methods, key punching, or some form of mechanical or optical scanning equipment. In large surveys, scanning is desirable because it scores questionnaires more quickly and accurately than any other approach.

A careful editing of each questionnaire is also necessary. The extent and complexity of this process depends on the type of scoring adopted and on the policy that is established to handle such problems as missing responses, careless coding, or extraneous marks. For example, if a questionnaire is scored by hand, it is usually unnecessary to inspect for extraneous marks since they will not be considered by the scorer. If, however, a survey is scored by an optical scanner, editing becomes a critical process because these marks may be erroneously read by the scanner as a response. Although this particular problem has been greatly reduced by modern scanners, which read responses only in predetermined positions, it is still very important to inspect each form.

Another editing problem occurs when a multiple choice item on a questionnaire is not answered or when two answers are given to the same question. At this point, the survey administrator must decide what constitutes a voided questionnaire. In many cases, it may be wise to treat any questionnaire on which a certain number of items are skipped as void and to eliminate it from further processing. In other cases, all items and all questionnaires are accepted, but separate counts of voids are recorded. While it is not possible to lay down hard-and-fast rules regarding these kinds of decisions, it is important for the survey administrator to establish a policy to deal with these problems before proceeding to the next stage of data processing.

ANALYSIS OF DATA

Analysis is the process of breaking down survey data into categories which are treated statistically or rearranged into meaningful patterns. Survey data can be quantitative or qualitative, and the analysis of each proceeds somewhat differently. Almost all surveys include multiple choice questions (those with fixed responses), which yield quantitative results. Many surveys also include interview results or comments written on questionnaires, which are qualitative in nature. Fixed response data represent static measures of job satisfaction or organizational health, while data compiled from comments and interviews can be more dynamic. The static measures deal with the effects (or at least their symptoms) of organizational problems, while the interview responses and written comments can help explain such effects and sometimes help to explain their causes.

Although questionnaires elicit fixed response data from all the respondents, interview and written comments may come from only a fraction of the participants because these responses are voluntary. Consequently, they often represent strong viewpoints. These two forms of data represent quite different inputs in survey analysis, and the distinction between them is quite useful for discussion purposes.

Analysis of questionnaire responses

Usually, fixed response data are analyzed with simple statistical indices such as mean scores or various response percentages. In some cases, responses to individual items are scored and analyzed, but more typically they are treated as parts of categories. In other cases, items are scored only as parts of an attitude scale, and only the total score is analyzed. Some examples of both treatments are shown in Figures 5.1 and 5.2. In Figure 5.1 the individual items are scored, but they are grouped according to the larger category to which they belong. Each item is presented in terms of its own norms. The level of job satisfaction found in the category as a whole is evaluated by the general trend of responses to individual items.

In Figure 5.2, however, the responses to individual items

FIGURE 5.1   Profile of Four Individually Scored Items Constituting a Given
                Category.

Friendliness and Cooperation of Fellow Employees					
Item	% Favorable	% Unfavorable	Centile Scale		
			20	40	60
The people I work with help each other out when someone falls behind or gets in a tight spot.	82	05			
A few of the people I work with think they run the place.	59	06			
The people I work with get along well together.	76	13			
The people I work with are very friendly.	85	09			

Source: Science Research Associates, Inc. (1962).

are incorporated into scales, and only the scaled scores are presented. In many programs, this approach is used in reporting the
responses to all core items. While reporting only the total scale
score causes some loss of detail, it is more reliable than reporting
scores of individual items. Thus, it provides a more stable measure of job satisfaction.

In many survey programs, a distinction is made between
core and supplemental items. As indicated, core items can form
carefully developed scales for which elaborate norms can be developed. The mean scores of each survey group are compared
with these norms. The supplemental items are also categorized
but are scored individually for each employee group, and the
resulting response percentages are simply reported. In many
cases this distinction implies a workable cause-and-effect
analysis, as discussed in Chapter Four. That is, the supplemental
items assess specific conditions in the organization that may
cause or contribute to job satisfaction while the scaled core items

FIGURE 5.2   Profile of a Single Scaled Score Made Up of Five
              Separate Items.

		Centiles		
	25	50	75	99
Co-workers	XXXXXXXXXXXXXXXXXX			

1. How do you generally feel about the employees you work with?

   They are the best group I could ask for
   I like them a great deal
   I like them fairly well
   I have no feeling one way or the other
   I don't particularly care for them

2. How is your *overall attitude* toward your job influenced by the
   people you work with?

   It is very favorably influenced
   It is favorably influenced
   It is not influenced one way or the other
   It is unfavorably influenced
   It is very unfavorably influenced

3. The example my fellow employees set

   greatly discourages me from working hard
   somewhat discourages me from working hard
   has little effect on me
   somewhat encourages me to work hard
   greatly encourages me to work hard

4. How much does the way co-workers handle their jobs add to the
   success of your department?

   It adds almost nothing
   It adds very little
   It adds only a little
   It adds quite a bit
   It adds a very great deal

5. In this unit, there is

   a very great deal of friction
   quite a bit of friction
   some friction
   little friction
   almost no friction

measure the effects of these conditions on job satisfaction. When supported by examples from written comments or interviews, even this kind of approximate analysis can be quite instructive for a manager.

Analysis of comments from questionnaires and interviews

Comments are treated as subjective information. They frequently represent the most intense feelings found within a group, and because the comments are usually expressed in personal terms, great care must be exercised to avoid revealing their individual sources when reporting them to management. In general, two approaches are usually used to analyze these kinds of survey data—a differential and an integrative approach.

Differential analysis • This approach, a form of simple content analysis, consists of placing each discrete comment either in preestablished categories or in categories that grow out of the analysis. Favorable and unfavorable comments are usually tallied separately; in certain cases, favorable comment categories are actually quite different from those used for unfavorable comments.

The following examples show how hypothetical negative comments could be categorized for tallying purposes under general headings.

Supervision

"Our boss checks on work endlessly. *He gives you an assignment and then checks on it every day until it is finished.*"

"My boss does not believe in delegation. *I don't think he could bring himself to let a subordinate assume any responsibility.*"

"Our manager does not seem concerned about us. He walks past my desk every day without even saying good morning."

"The bosses here treat people like school kids. *They want to watch each move we make.*"

"Talking to the office manager is like talking to a wall.

I guess she feels we don't know as much as she does, *so we should not be taken seriously."*

"Our office manager seems nice, and will listen to you when you talk to her, but she never acts on a suggestion."

"It doesn't do any good to ask our office manager a question. She says she will get back to you, but she never does."

"You can't talk to our office manager about anything. *Your boss will know about it before you get back to your desk."*

"You can't talk to our office manager about anything confidential. She tells everything to her cronies and it is all over the office before you get back to your desk."

"Management acts as if they don't trust us. You can't even be a minute late and we have exactly one hour for lunch."

"My boss never lets me do a job the way I think it could be done. It's always his way."

"My boss is very insensitive to employee feelings. He is very sarcastic and abusive."

Kind of work

"My job is boring. It's the same old thing day after day. I can do much more than I am allowed to do."

"I do all kinds of things that have nothing to do with what I was hired for. My boss even has me run errands for him. Sometimes I can't even finish my work."

"We are never given information for the things we do. Everything is treated as a big, dark secret and we aren't allowed in on the act."

"I don't feel responsible for anything I do. All of the work is parceled out in small pieces. *It seems as though it was designed so that we would not be able to see the whole project or know what it is all about."*

Amount of work

"There's always too much to do at my desk. I have more than enough to do—and the worst part is my neighbor sits all day talking on the phone while I work my head off. Why can't they see that she's not busy and give her some of my workload?"

"The workload goes in spurts around here. I can sit for

days on end doing nothing. Then all of a sudden there's more than I can handle—all of it due immediately. You'd think my bosses could plan so I didn't get everything at the last minute."

Co-workers

"She gets away with everything. I can't be two minutes late from lunch and I get yelled at. She can be gone half the day and nobody says a word. If there have to be rules, they should be the same for everyone."

"Some of the people I work with take great care in reporting everything to the boss. *Management shouldn't encourage this kind of tattle-tale behavior.*"

Physical surroundings

"The desks in the office are arranged like a school-room. *Perhaps it allows the boss to keep an eye on people,* but it is a very uncomfortable arrangement."

"The lounge areas do not allow any privacy."

"I don't like the way desks are arranged in the department. It makes it almost impossible to talk to the people in front of you and this is frequently necessary. *It almost reminds me of a schoolroom.*"

Financial rewards

"There seems to be a great deal of secrecy about our pay around here. *Apparently management does not want one person to know that they are paid more than another.* I don't feel this is right."

If the number of comments is large and varied enough, the categories can be further subdivided to refine the analysis. By simply tallying the number and nature of comments in each category or subcategory, a rough analysis can be accomplished.

Differential analysis has several advantages. It can be performed by relatively untrained people and can summarize a large number of comments rather quickly. Moreover, it provides a general indication of the extent of various organizational problems and a general measure of employees' opinions about different organizational conditions. A further refinement of the procedure can allow for the tallying of both the content and the intensity of comments. In this way, not only is the frequency of comments in a given subject area assessed, but those categories with strongly phrased comments can be highlighted. At the same time, because the very process of separating comments into different categories tends to destroy some of their feeling and tone and tends to obscure the similarities among them, it is often advisable to integrate the data by searching for themes within it.

Integrative analysis • This subjective approach can also be carried out by nonprofessionals, but it takes skill and experience. Although there are several established techniques for the analysis of individual comments, most of these are based on specific theories of personality and require the aid of highly trained people. In everyday survey work, however, the data collected are not highly personal in nature, and any in-depth analysis would be inappropriate. Moreover, survey data is, by definition, group data. The approach usually taken, therefore, is simply to review the comments for common threads of meaning or association. Because many comments directed at specific areas reflect a more general or underlying theme, such an analysis is often quite meaningful. For example, individual comments about a wide range of subjects frequently reflect employees' distrust of management. (This is, in fact, one of the themes among the comments listed above and is indicated by the segments in italics.)

Because the process of categorizing items tends to destroy continuity, a search for themes is not usually conducted if the comments have already been categorized. By searching the comments and interview results of each employee for themes, a common problem of categorized data can be avoided. For example, when one or two employees make many comments that are placed in several different categories according to their content, administrators can mistake the similar tone of these comments for a general theme. This error can be avoided if all the comments of individual employees are given identifying numbers or are coded in some way. In the analysis of one large survey of executives, the individual comments of twenty thousand people were numbered, coded, and typed on an optical scan format. Seventy thousand comments were recorded this way. As a result, items on any subject could be called from the data bank at any time and could be subjected to either a differential or an integrative analysis.

Themes do not always exist in comment data, nor are they always readily apparent. When themes do appear, however, their identification can help management understand survey results. It is strongly suggested, therefore, that a thematic search be routinely conducted.

Protection of anonymity • Great care should be exercised when reporting comments to managers in order to preserve the anonymity of the respondents. Many survey administrators provide managers with narrative summaries of comments rather than reports on each comment. Moreover, only narrative summaries of *group* opinions are reported rather than those of extremely small minorities. The problem with reporting individual comments as they are written or minority opinions is that peculiarities of expression in many comments, especially if the remarks happen to be critical, may allow a manager to identify, or perhaps even mistakenly identify, a survey respondent. (In fact, the name of the game often played by some managers is "guess who said that.") Even a well-intentioned manager may be tempted in such an instance to act vindictively or in a biased manner. To the extent that managers are encouraged or tempted to take action against people rather than their problems, the survey has failed. Thus, single or infrequent comments should not be reported. Although this involves the loss of some data, it seems a small price to pay to maintain the integrity of the survey program.

An exception to this rule occurs when respondents are told ahead of time that their comments will be reported exactly as they are written to management. In some cases, employees are encouraged to write comments they actually want management to see and perhaps recognize. This approach does relieve the administrator of any responsibility for protecting the confidentiality of responses, but it also seems to jeopardize one of the strengths of the survey approach, the guarantee of anonymity to survey participants.

Comments as a source of new survey questions • A frequently overlooked value of comments from interviews or questionnaires is their use as a source of new items for surveys. As times and conditions change, the content of survey instruments should change as well. For the survey administrator who intends to maintain a survey program, a file of comments from previous surveys can be invaluable in replacing, rewriting, or adding items to an instrument.

INTERPRETATION OF DATA

The interpretation of survey data is an attempt to make sense of the raw results produced by the analysis and to point out their organizational implications to management. It is both an art and a science. In order to interpret survey data, administrators must exercise professional judgment. They must be knowledgeable about organizational processes and certain mechanical procedures. In some instances, additional investigation through interviews and group discussion techniques may also be required to fully understand the results.

Relative nature of interpretation

Most results yielded by survey analyses should be interpreted in a relative manner. As indicated in Chapter Four, norms may be constructed for different dimensions of the work environment, such as occupational groups, demographic classifications, or regional or administrative locations. By comparing the results of any given group to appropriate norms, a more meaningful interpretation can be made. Norms can be defined on the basis of these classifications within an organization or in terms of their representation in the general workforce. In most cases, in-house programs develop norms solely from within the organization while programs offered by survey consultants develop norms from survey results in many organizations.

It is possible to develop a survey without using any established norms. In such instances, the results provide descriptive information that may help management understand a particular problem or situation. Usually, this involves a comparison of one group to others within the organization. While workable, this procedure has a basic weakness, which is illustrated by the following example of a survey conducted in a hospital. Scores were determined for each function and department in the hospital. In the absence of any other standard, a strictly internal comparison was made, and the satisfaction levels for each function were determined. The fact that some occupational groups in hospitals *typically* have higher levels of satisfaction than others was overlooked. Thus, it was of little value to know only that the nursing staff was more satisfied than the housekeeping staff. A more meaningful analysis would also have shown how the nursing staff compared to nursing staffs at other hospitals. In this particular case, management was actually lulled into the belief that the nursing group had no serious problems when, in fact, a subsequent study showed that from a normative point of view, the nurses were the least satisfied employees in the hospital.[1]

Use of results from past surveys

One additional advantage of an ongoing survey program is that survey results can be compared with data from earlier surveys. When such scores exist, they add greatly to interpretive power. The survey administrator should not attach much importance to minor changes or to those based on scores of small groups since these are likely to represent chance variations. In many established programs the differences are automatically tested for statistical significance in order to rule out unwarranted interpretations.

Figure 5.3 presents a profile of a typical unit, showing present and past survey results. This comparison reflects changes in both directions in the eight categories. It gives the manager a much better understanding of the level of job satisfaction in the unit than the current scores alone. These scores can provide managers with valuable indices of a higher level of job satisfaction or of incipient problems among a group of employees.

Trends developed in this same way, but over a longer period of time, can be even more useful in monitoring reactions to changes in organizational direction or policy. Figure 5.4 presents an example of a twelve-year study of one attitudinal category (supervision) that involved three different occupational groups. By indicating changing strengths and weaknesses in an organization, this long-term comparison can be helpful to managers. For example, the results presented in Figure 5.4 clearly indicate that satisfaction deteriorated in Group A while it improved in Group B and changed irregularly in Group C. By knowing where and

1. *In certain cases, it is possible to achieve an "absolute" interpretation of survey data by using an "intensity analysis." Although a complete description of this approach would be inappropriate here, the interested reader is referred to Guttman (1947), Suchman (1950), or to a summary treatment by Torgerson (1958). This technique allows for the establishment of an approximate "zero" point for attitude scales that meet certain psychometric criteria. Once such a point has been fixed, it provides a means of interpreting attitudinal data in absolute terms.*

FIGURE 5.3   Profile of 1974 and 1977 Results for Total Unit.

Satisfaction Facet		No. Resp.	Degree of Employee Satisfaction and Motivation		
			Low	Neutral	High
Supervision					
	Overall	305		XXXXXXXXXXXX	
	Previous Survey 74	300		0000	
Kind of Work	Previous Survey 74	305		XXXXXX	
				000000	
Amount of Work	Previous Survey 74	304	XXXX		
				0000	
Co-workers	Previous Survey 74	306		XXXXXX	
			00000000		
Physical Surroundings	Previous Survey 74	305	XXXX		
				000	
Financial Rewards	Previous Survey 74	305		XXXXXXXXX	
			000		
Career Future and Security	Previous Survey 74	305		XXXXXXXXXXXXX	
				0000	
Company Identification		305		XXXXXXXXXXXX	
				0000000000	

how these changes occurred, management was in a much better position to take intelligent corrective action. When the probable causal factors for these trends are highlighted, the interpretation becomes even more convincing. The identification of such causal factors may require additional qualitative information regarding specific influences. In other instances, a professional survey administrator's experience with similar situations may suggest the causes for the change.

FIGURE 5.4   Longitudinal Study of Three Work Groups: Supervisory Category.

Category	Year	Group	N	Centile Scale (corporate wide) 1 25 50 75 99
Supervision	1963	A	(4802)	
		B	(6080)	
		C	(3712)	
	1967	A	(4380)	
		B	(6004)	
		C	(3600)	
	1974	A	(4008)	
		B	(5930)	
		C	(3550)	

Identification of group influences

Numerous factors that affect group reactions have been isolated by social research and organizational experience. Examples of two such influences are discussed here.

Reference groups • One of the well-established findings in the field of social psychology is that feelings of satisfaction and group well-being are strongly influenced by various reference groups (see the discussion of equity theory in Chapter Two). That is, outside groups are used as points of comparison by members of a given organization. Thus, in order to understand the attitudes of a group, it is often necessary to identify their reference group. Quite naturally, such influences are encountered frequently in interpreting survey results. The profiles of two similar work groups in one company are compared in Figures 5.5 and 5.6.

At first glance, the results suggest that these two groups had almost identical reactions to their physical surroundings. However, a review of the two locations by industrial engineers

FIGURE 5.5   Profile of Service Technicians in Unit 1.

Satisfaction Facet		No. Resp.	Degree of Employee Satisfaction and Motivation		
			Low	Neutral	High
Supervision					
	Mgr.				XXXXXXXXXXXX
	Asst. Mgr.				XXXXXX
	Pers. Mgr.				XXXXXXXXXX
	Sup.				XXXX
Kind of Work					XXXXXXXXXXXX
Amount of Work					XX
Co-workers					XXXXXXXXXXXXXX
Physical Surroundings				XXXXXXXX	
Financial Rewards				XXXXXXXXXX	
Career Future and Security			XXXXXXXXXXXXXX		
Company Identification				XXXXXXXXX	

FIGURE 5.6 Profile of Service Technicians in Unit 2.

Satisfaction Facet		No. Resp.	Degree of Employee Satisfaction and Motivation		
			Low	Neutral	High
Supervision					
	Mgr.		XXXXXXXXXX		
	Asst. Mgr.		XXXXXXXXXXXX		
	Pers. Mgr.			XXXXXX	
	Sup.			XX	
Kind of Work					XXXXXXXXXX
Amount of Work					XXX
Co-workers					XXXXXXXXXX
Physical Surroundings				XXXXXXXX	
Financial Rewards					
Career Future and Security					XXXXXXXXXXXXXXX
Company Identification					XXXXXXX

indicated that there were significant differences between them. In the first situation (Unit 1), the physical surroundings were deficient in a number of ways, and the company was planning to upgrade them regardless of the results of the survey. In the second situation (Unit 2), the physical surroundings seemed to be well above average engineering standards.

When interviews and discussions were conducted for the two groups, it was found that different influences were at work. Not surprisingly, the attitudes of employees in Unit 1 stemmed directly from specific substandard conditions in their work environment. Almost all employees in Unit 2, however, were dissatisfied because another organization provided better facilities for people doing the same work. This apparent reference group phenomenon indicated that the employees in Unit 2 felt deprived in relation to another group. By pointing out the real nature of the problem, it was possible to have management understand and accept it. As a result, managers were better able to take the feelings and perceptions of employees into consideration along with the results of the objective engineering study.

Buffer groups • Another example of an interpretive technique that can lend further meaning to results is the buffer group phenomenon. The term refers to a group of people who occupy an intermediate position between two levels in an organization and who use this position to alter the influence of one level on the other. The profiles shown in Figures 5.7 and 5.8 were obtained from two different groups—supervisors and their subordinates (salespeople)—in the same unit. As can be seen, supervisors had negative attitudes toward their superiors, the unit managers, while the attitudes of their subordinates, the salespeople, were positive toward almost all levels of supervision.

Initially, such findings may be puzzling. The results could have been an indication that the supervisors' dissatisfaction had only recently emerged and had not yet been felt by subordinates. In this case, rather quick action would have been required to prevent the dissatisfaction from spreading.

On the other hand, as was the case in this example, interviews among supervisors showed that the problem had existed for a long time. They believed that the quality of management in

FIGURE 5.7   Profile of Supervisors.

Satisfaction Facet		No. Resp.	Degree of Employee Satisfaction and Motivation		
			Low	Neutral	High
Supervision					
	Mgr.	45		XXXXXXX	
	Asst. Mgr.	45		XXXX	
	Merch. Mgr.	45			X
	Pers. Mgr.	45		XXX	
	Controller	45		XX	
Kind of Work		45			XXXXXXXX
Amount of Work		45		XXXX	
Co-workers		45			XXXXXXXXXX
Physical Surroundings		45			XX
Financial Rewards		45			XXXX
Career Future and Security		45			XX
Company Identification		45			XXXXXXX

FIGURE 5.8   Profile of Salespeople.

Satisfaction Facet		No. Resp.	Degree of Employee Satisfaction and Motivation		
			Low	Neutral	High
Supervision					
	Mgr.				XXXXXX
	Asst. Mgr.				XX
	Merch. Mgr.			XXX	
	Pers. Mgr.			XXXX	
	Controller			XX	
	Sup.				XXXXXXX
Kind of Work				XXX	
Amount of Work			X		
Co-workers					XXXXXXXXX
Physical Surroundings				XXX	
Financial Rewards				XXXXX	
Career Future and Security				XXXX	
Company Identification					XXXXXXX

their unit had steadily deteriorated during the past few years and that managers were treating them in an increasingly harsh and unreasonable way. It was also discovered that the supervisors were an especially close-knit group and took great pride in their unit, where many had worked for years. These factors had led supervisors to act as a line of defense, or buffer group, between unit managers and salespeople. Their apparent pride in the operation and their career commitment to the organization not only led them to accept whatever pressure was being exerted on them from above but also to prevent it from being "passed on down the line." In this particular case, the supervisors were really the backbone of the organization.

In general, interpretation of survey results is a mixture of objective and subjective processes. If it is based on sound professional experience and carefully developed data analyses, interpretation can make survey information "come alive" by pointing out its behavioral and organizational implications. Thus, it is an essential process because it helps management to understand survey data and act on results in an intelligent and timely fashion.

REPORTING SURVEY RESULTS

In large organizations, survey data are reported at several levels, and to make this process effective, some preliminary decisions must be made. In general, they should be based on the kind of interest and organizational action the survey results are likely to produce. Each group of participants in a survey—the top executives who sponsor it, the local managers who administer or arrange for it, and the employees who take it—has a particular interest in certain results and can be the focus or the agent of appropriate followup action. Results, therefore, should be presented to all three organizational groups but should be concentrated at levels where interest is high.

While the following two sections offer advice on how to report results to management, it should be remembered that it is also essential to present this information to employees. (The feedback process is examined later in the chapter. The importance of integrating information presented to management and to employees is also discussed in the same section.)

Reporting results to top executives

The cardinal rule in reporting survey results to top executives is to summarize the results so they can be understood, but to present them so candidly that they cannot be misunderstood. This takes knowledge and technical competence and often a great deal of courage! It requires knowledge of the organization to decide which results should be referred to the corporate level, and it requires skill to organize these results effectively. When these results are critical of an organization, it takes considerable courage on the part of the survey administrator to report them candidly. To be less than candid, however, is to do a disservice to employees, management, and the organization.

It takes less courage to present favorable results to top executives, but it is equally important to report them as well. It is vital that top executives understand which company policies and practices are endorsed by employees as well as which ones are criticized. Such information may prevent management from inadvertently changing a well-accepted policy while trying to correct a related but criticized one—a classic case of throwing the baby out with the bathwater. It is for these reasons that the commitment of top executives to hear *all* the survey results and to act on them constructively is so important.

In general, results pertaining to corporate goals, policies, practices, and philosophies should be the focus of the report to the top levels of management. General trends and significant variations in results between geographic regions, administrative units, or demographic groupings should be included in the report, but these results should be condensed and presented in summary form. (Although it may take the survey administrator or consultant months to compile a report to executives, they will have only a limited amount of time to digest it before turning attention to some other subject.)[2] In this regard, visual displays of data can be very helpful in summarizing large amounts of information. Two examples are shown in Figures 5.9 and 5.10.

Note that in Figure 5.9, a very large amount of data was made almost immediately comprehensible by a visual display of the results. By presenting the above-average, average, and below-average scores of each group on each scale as different shaded areas, the problem and nonproblem groups can be seen at a glance. In Figure 5.10, the general strengths and weaknesses associated with one category of organizational health, supervision, are apparent. When compared to the average score for supervision for all work groups in the company (shown by the gray shaded bar), the relative standing of each group can be readily understood.

Reporting results to managers

In most surveys, the majority of the findings will focus on job satisfaction issues at local levels of the organization. Supervisory practices, pay administration, career advancement, working conditions, and interpersonal relationships are but a few of the frequently mentioned areas. Unlike the executive, who is usually more interested in general trends, the local manager al-

2. *Executives, however, often expect to examine survey results in detail. Survey administrators should be prepared to answer the requests for elaboration, clarification, and explanation of survey results that frequently arise in meetings with executives.*

FIGURE 5.9   Reactions of Nine Work Groups to Their Present Work Assignments.

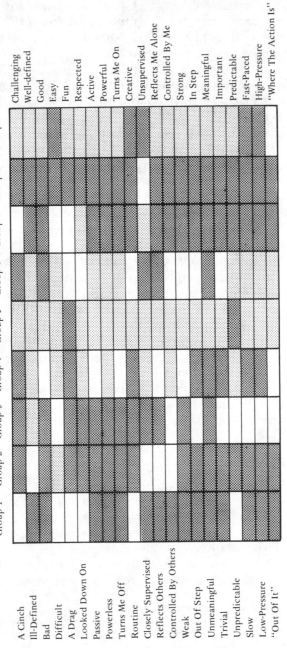

FIGURE 5.10   Scores of Ten Key Work Groups in the Supervisory Category.

Group		Degree of Employee Satisfaction and Motivation		
		Low	Neutral	High
1	50			
2	67			
3	35			
4	21			
5	45			
6	40			
7	52			
8	401			
9	376			
10	107			

Corporate Average

ways needs a detailed explanation of how employees respond to each dimension of the work environment.

Thus, survey administrators should present local managers with the most detailed information possible without compromising the anonymity of the respondents. By establishing the ground rules for reporting survey results ahead of time, accuracy and confidentiality can be achieved. For example, profiles, which are based on group averages, can be prepared for groups of five or more people. This minimum allows meaningful results to be presented for relatively small groups but does not identify individual respondents.

When reporting group response percentages, however, a different minimum can be established to protect anonymity. Only rounded or broad percentage figures (e.g., 10 or 20 percent) should be used and only for groups of fifteen or more. (This rule discourages the inadvertent highlighting of one respondent's results that would occur by reporting that 10 percent of ten people, for example, hold a certain viewpoint.)

Figures 5.11 and 5.12 demonstrate this form of reporting. These profiles are typical of those included in a survey report.

FIGURE 5.11   Profile of Salespeople.

Satisfaction Facet		No. Resp.	Degree of Employee Satisfaction and Motivation		
			Low	Neutral	High
Supervision					
	Mgr.	21		XXXX	
	Asst. Mgr.	20		X	
	Mgr. (1)	18		XXXXXXX	
	Mgr. (2)	16		XXX	
	Pers. Mgr.	3			
Kind of Work		21		XXX	
Amount of Work		20			
Co-workers		21		XXXXXXX	
Physical Surroundings		19		XXX	
Financial Rewards		20		XXXXX	
Career Future and Security		21		XXX	
Company Identification		22		XXXXXXXXXX	

They represent the average score of each employee group in eight different areas of job satisfaction. In the supervisory area, the scores are subdivided to reflect attitudes toward each of the important managers. Notice that in Figure 5.11, no results were obtained for one supervisor (the personnel manager) since less than five people responded, while for other supervisors, with whom employees were more familiar, results were obtained. In Figure 5.12, which depicts the percentages of responses to individual descriptive items, the responses of members of the Office group were also eliminated since less than fifteen people answered these questions. It should be noted that in both cases, employee responses were not totally eliminated. Rather, they appeared in profiles and reports that were based on combinations of these smaller groups.

Since the majority of survey data can be expected to relate to local situations, the report prepared for management at the local level is likely to be quite lengthy. Thus, careful organization of its contents is especially important. For an ongoing survey program, this can and probably should result in some type of

FIGURE 5.12   Response Percentages for Five Work Groups: Descriptive Items.

	Employee Groups					
	Total	Sup.	Sales	Non sup.	Office	Wrhse.
	345	42	106	129	10	58
Personnel Manager shows great deal of interest in the way things go in our store	70	85	75	70		60
Negative response	30	15	25	30		40
Personnel Manager helps people with their problems	65	75	65	65		55
Negative response	35	25	35	35		45
Find it easy to discuss problems with Personnel Manager	85	90	90	90		60
Negative response	15	10	10	10		40
Personnel Manager follows up on employee questions	60	75	55	70		50
Negative response	40	25	45	30		50

standardized report format. This approach facilitates the processing of large amounts of survey data and makes the report easier for managers to understand. Through repeated exposures to survey reports, managers become more familiar with their structure and develop a high degree of competence in interpreting their contents.

To facilitate this learning process, the report should have a structure that is meaningful and easy to understand. This starts with the logical ordering of responses to related items. All items in a given category should be placed together. The ordering of survey items concerning supervision represents the most obvious example. Not only should such items be grouped in one section of the report, but they should be arranged to describe different established dimensions of leadership. Thus, those items that deal with task-oriented and with interpersonal leadership behavior should be placed together. Because this arrangement is standardized, it is possible to supplement this section of the report with a fairly elaborate description of each of these leadership dimensions.

The predetermined format of the supervisory section provides local managers with both a meaningful summary of the leadership in their units and a basis for a functional supervisory training program. That is, a manager can use the results as a basis for diagnosing a unit's supervisory strengths and weaknesses as well as for educational discussions with supervisory personnel. The data on supervision provided by employees in the supervisor's unit can be compared to the more general and theoretical descriptions of leadership behavior included in the report. As a result, the discussion of supervisory behavior takes on a very realistic tone because it is based on employees' perceptions in a given unit.

The content of other categories can also be organized to reflect their various dimensions. Responses to questions about work rewards can be arranged to reflect attitudes toward both financial and nonfinancial factors. Survey data on career development can be prepared to reflect attitudes toward job security and job advancement.

FEEDBACK TO EMPLOYEES

Employees usually want to know what the results of a survey are and what impact they have on effecting changes in organizational policies. A successful reporting of results to respondents depends on how well the other parts of the program are designed and implemented and on how well the feedback process itself is designed and monitored. Because surveys measure the level of organizational well-being and serve as vehicles for employee participation to improve it, the feedback process is the heart of the program.

While an active and long-term feedback approach is recommended, it should be recognized that in some situations survey feedback has to be carried out within time constraints and cannot be part of an ongoing organizational effort. In surveys of project groups, for instance, the short life of the project may preclude an elaborate or continued feedback program. Even here, however, surveys can be of great help in improving the present project or in designing the next.

In an active feedback program, survey results are reported to employees to encourage them to participate in groups designed to improve organizational effectiveness. (This problem-solving approach is discussed in the last section of this chapter.) In a passive feedback program, however, the results are reported simply to convey information. A survey that measures group attitudes on a particular economic, political, or social issue is of this type. However, most organizations have adopted some type of active and continuous approach to the feedback process. These are the approaches described in this section.

Nature of the feedback process

After managers receive the survey report, they should implement the feedback process as soon as possible. The procedure described here assumes that managers rather than consultants are responsible for carrying out the feedback process. If consultants are used, managers are usually less involved, but they should still accept responsibility for the results.

Sequence of feedback sessions • The sequence for feedback reports depends on the structure of the organization. In most cases, managers report the general findings to their own management staffs before presenting them to first-level supervisors and to employee groups. Because the survey report itself may later serve as a basis for a very detailed analysis of the whole operation and its leadership, the management staff will normally expect a discussion of any significant points that affect them or their operations. Certainly, any salient points that will be presented in the general feedback sessions to all employees should be covered beforehand in the session with the management staff.

Next, managers meet with the first-level supervisors. In many cases, they will have participated as respondents in the survey, and in such instances, this meeting represents the first respondent feedback session. Managers may want to give detailed feedback to supervisors, including the results that pertain to them as well as to their subordinates. It also provides a good opportunity for the manager to enlist supervisors' support in the feedback and followup program that will take place among their subordinates. If supervisors can be shown the benefit of the survey and the changes that result from it, they are much more likely to convey a favorable and supportive attitude to their subordinates.

Structure and content of the feedback report • The feedback to each employee group should cover all pertinent areas in the survey report. That is, while members of each group should be given a general overview of the results for the entire organization, the report should focus on the findings that are especially relevant to them. In most cases, the report should be written and should be read to participants to insure that all points are covered (a written summary may also be of interest). The feedback report usually includes a

1) brief introduction. This includes an expression of appreciation to respondents for their participation, a brief explanation of when and why the survey was carried out, and an endorsement of the program by the manager. If the report is to be read, it is helpful to comment on the reason for reading it rather than discussing it informally. A suggested approach might be, "I hope you will pardon me if I read this report to you. As you know, the survey dealt with a number of areas and I want to make sure I cover all of them."

2) statement of favorable areas. It is usually best to begin with the areas that received favorable responses to let people know that the focus of the session is not on negative points only. In fact, a common misconception of employees and management is that surveys are only concerned with problem areas. The majority of surveys yield a balance of praise and criticism about the organization, and a responsible manager will want to present both sides. Organizational strengths are of equal or greater importance than weaknesses and should be emphasized in feedback sessions.

3) statement of mixed areas. In most surveys, there are categories that receive a balanced reaction of positive and negative feelings and others that receive, on the average, responses of mild approval or disapproval. It is important to explain to respondents that there are differences of opinion on some issues and that others are not of major concern to most people in the organization.

4) statement of negative areas. This is frequently the most difficult area for managers to handle, since they are likely to be sensitive to any criticism of their units or operations. It is important that all such areas are covered, however, because any attempt to avoid them may cause

resentment among respondents. (Several suggestions on how to handle some of the most sensitive problems appear later in the chapter.)

5) <u>statement of planned actions.</u> Respondents want to learn the results of a survey, but frequently they are more interested in knowing what actions will result. Therefore, managers should indicate which actions they can and will take, which actions they can but will not take, which actions will have to be taken by managers at a higher level, and which actions will require the cooperation of both managers and employees. Usually, the most immediate action that managers take in response to survey results involves a tangible aspect of the work situation or one that is most important to many respondents. Other actions may take more time and money, but it is very important to communicate any contemplated actions in the feedback session. In addition, actions desired by employees which cannot be initiated for economic or other reasons should be communicated along with the explanations of why such actions cannot be carried out. This will not please most respondents, but people generally accept a straight answer if it is explained reasonably.

6) <u>call for discussion.</u> The preceding steps involve one-way or downward communication. If this information is presented in an authoritarian manner, the survey feedback process can disintegrate into a passive reception of information by employees. This, of course, defeats the main purpose of survey feedback. By requesting questions and encouraging discussion of the points raised in the report, managers can prevent this problem.

Number of feedback meetings • The employees who attend the feedback sessions should have some common interest in the findings. It is recommended, therefore, that managers conduct feedback sessions for work groups with related functions. For example, in an organization of three or four hundred people, a manager may conduct as many as twenty to twenty-five feedback meetings. Although managers must prepare separate feedback reports for the various functional groups, the added effectiveness is worth the extra time and effort. The survey administrator can contribute to the effectiveness of these individual feedback meetings by arranging the survey report to allow easy access to data on each group. If the report is divided into appropriate sections for each functional work group, managers can simply refer to each section when preparing their own feedback reports.

The consensus among managers who have tried this approach is that the meetings have resulted in exchanges of information that are interesting to both employees and managers. In many cases, survey feedback has merely served as a vehicle for initiating this type of communication. In fact, many managers have elected to hold similar meetings on a continuing basis.

The atmosphere of the feedback session • The manager's behavior is of crucial importance in creating an appropriate atmosphere for the feedback meeting. Establishing an open and constructive environment for feedback meetings is by far the most important ingredient in achieving success. This can be done in a number of ways. First, the meeting should be held for only one purpose. It should not involve any business or subject other than the reporting and discussion of survey results. Second, the seating arrangements should be as informal as possible and should avoid a schoolroom appearance. The manager's office may often be better than a conference room for such a meeting if it is large enough to accommodate the feedback group. Refreshments can also contribute to the climate. In addition, the manager should allot sufficient time for the meeting and not appear rushed or preoccupied with other concerns. The manager should view the meeting as a learning experience and treat it as a real opportunity to discuss the strengths and weaknesses of the organization.

The following list offers some other suggestions that the manager might observe when conducting a feedback meeting.

a) Avoid a defensive posture when dealing with criticism. This will encourage discussion. Managers who can accept criticism or suggestions about their units usually generate a great deal of respect and are likely to open up important channels of communication with their subordinates. This is not to suggest that managers must agree with or act upon all critical comments, but they should treat them as a valid and valuable source of information. Trying to dismiss an observation reported in a survey is unwise and usually stifles the discussion. It should be remembered that human perceptions rather than objective facts are reported in a survey. These perceptions often determine behavior; they are valid in the minds of the individual respondents regardless of whether they are, in fact, accurate or inaccurate.

b) The use of humor can contribute greatly to the ideal climate in a feedback meeting. It relieves tension and can be an effective means of dealing with difficult situations. If it is directed at individuals or used as a way of dismissing problems, however, it actually becomes dysfunctional. This point is often overlooked by managers who are uncomfortable discussing a given section of the survey report. In an effort to release their own tensions, they are likely to resort to some joking comment or sarcastic remark.

c) Managers should avoid treating any subject area as frivolous. The fact that it was highlighted in the survey report indicates that it represents the attitudes of a substantial group of people. If these results are dismissed or treated as a minor issue, employees may feel that managers are talking down to them or shutting them off.

d) A real effort should be made to treat criticism of management or the management staff as constructive information. Managers should neither apologize for nor defend their leadership: they should attempt to face the issue directly. In doing so, it is not necessary to describe the details of the criticisms or the personalities of the supervisors involved. In fact, it would be as great a mistake to identify staff members who may have been criticized as it would be to ignore the subject altogether. However, the general subject can be discussed to show employees that their complaints have been heard and are being seriously considered.

The statements of one manager who had received some criticism in a survey represent one successful way of treating this problem. He handled his feedback session in the following way:

I do want to tell you that there was a good deal of criticism of your supervision in the report. Some of this was directed at me as well as the staff, and I want you to know I am especially concerned about it. After reviewing the findings, however, I became aware of how some of our behavior could be misunderstood and in some cases resented. Now that I understand this, I can assure you that this was not our intent, and I can also assure you that a real effort will be made to correct it. I won't go into details, other than to give you an example. Over the past year I have asked each staff person to tour the store each day. The purpose of this was to make staff people available to you and to provide help when needed. I think this is very necessary and important, but what has happened is that these visits became inspections and most of our comments during them turned out to be critical of your operations. This was not our intent, but I realize the complaint is valid. I have fallen into the same habit myself.

I have given this considerable thought and I want you to know that your criticism may have helped us all. I want to assure you that you can expect to see some improvement starting now. After all, whenever some member of the staff or I sit down with each of you to review your performance, we are sometimes critical of some things you have done. We do this in order to bring about improvement. Well, now, you had your chance to review our performance and we'd be fools if we didn't try to profit from it. Hopefully, our next survey will show we have. In the meantime, I want to thank you for being candid in your comments about supervision in this survey.

Managers should cover every subject area of the survey, but they should avoid going into detail. The only exceptions to this general rule are areas of employee concern or enthusiasm. If employees are very critical of a particular organizational policy or condition, their comments should certainly receive more than general mention because they may generate some suggestions for improvement or corrective action. These suggestions, in turn, can be reported as part of the feedback process.

Areas of organizational strength should also be discussed in detail to help employees and managers understand the sources of these strengths. For example, an organizational program, such as a production run or a sales effort, may require much effort and planning to be successful. If it later receives praise from employees in a survey, managers could use the opportunity to explain how and why the program worked so well and to thank employees for their help. In this way, an important educational step would be taken, and the groundwork would be established for the next effort.

FEEDBACK AS A PROBLEM-SOLVING APPROACH

In general, the procedures described to this point have stressed management's role in the feedback process. However, the feedback of survey data also can be used to generate problem-solving efforts which capitalize on employee participation.[3] In fact, the initial feedback session and subsequent discussion is often the first step in an action-oriented followup program in which employees and managers frequently work together to solve many of the problems that the survey uncovers.

Managers should clearly decide which actions they can take alone, which actions must be left to their superiors, and which ones will require the cooperation of employees and management. Once this has been decided and communicated, management can then initiate any one of several programs.

Followup committees

The traditional and most effective way of acting on survey results is to form committees to work on specific problems. Membership should include people in the organization who are interested in or responsible for a given problem area. The number, size, and membership of committees is limited by the number of problems and the time and resources that management and employees are willing and able to spend.

Committee action should focus on the work environment. Too often, committees attempt to solve problems, especially those of an interpersonal nature, by devising programs that bring people together for various activities during nonwork hours. Supervisory training meetings, athletic programs, or purely social events are common examples. While bowling teams and pic-

3. See Filley (1975) for a detailed discussion of this issue.

nics and other such activities can be very successful from the participant's point of view, and should be encouraged, they may have little effect on behavior at work. Whenever it is possible, therefore, committees should strive to solve work-related problems within the work environment.

Timetables for meetings and reporting progress should also be established for committees. Scheduling problems and the absence of timetables for accomplishing goals often dissipate the enthusiasm of many committees.

Nominal groups

The Nominal Group Technique (NGT) has been used for many years in many different settings.[4] NGT is essentially an unstructured means for getting people to effectively use the resources of the group to solve a problem. In the early stage of the process, the members of a Nominal Group work by themselves to devise solutions. This stage capitalizes on the increased productivity of individual effort and insures that all members participate equally. Later, the members form small groups to critically examine each of the solutions that were generated privately. Attempts are then made to agree upon a priority of proposed solutions to the problem. The small groups later merge into one large group to establish final priorities.

Because NGT is relatively easy to manage, it has become quite popular as a means of defining and solving problems. In some cases, NGT is used as a survey approach itself, but its tendency to focus on one problem area at a time limits its value as a survey technique. This, however, can become an advantage when the NGT is used as a followup to a complete survey. In other words, a survey usually explores a broad range of problems in an organization and provides some sense of their relative importance. Once this is established, the NGT can be used to concentrate attention on one or two of the most pressing problems. Together, the two techniques make maximum use of the survey's ability to diagnose problems and the NGT's ability to determine an ordered set of solutions.

---

4. Delbecq, Van de Ven, and Gustafson (1975) have provided a clear, concise explanation of NGT.

The NGT seems to be well suited to solve problems that affect an entire unit or organization, such as the lack of communication between shifts or departments, inadequate training of new employees, explanations of new procedures, or friction between groups. In these situations, representatives of each subgroup in the organization can form the Nominal Group. For problems that affect only one or two small functional groups, such as bottlenecks in workflow, lack of cooperation between subgroups, or inefficiencies in the layout of a particular work place, all members of each group can participate in the Nominal Group exercise.

Feedback in training programs

The survey feedback process can also be used as a method of training managers. In one organization, data are collected on a periodic basis, feedback sessions are conducted, and goals are established for achieving improvements in satisfaction. In order to reach these goals, however, local managers must be responsive to the problems of subordinates and must be competent to deal with those problems. Thus, the organization has established a systematic training program to help managers develop the necessary skills. The training includes modeling and reinforcement techniques which identify and reward the utilization of correct managerial processes and subsequent problem-solving. The system, which is supported by the top levels of management, is used as a basis for the management of satisfaction. (Dodd and Pesci, 1977).

Integration of feedback among organizational levels

Each level of an organization should be informed about the results that have been reported to other levels. In this way, a further integration of the reporting and feedback systems occurs. For example, survey results pertaining to a company policy such as an employee benefit program would be primarily reported to top executives because only they can make changes in corporate policy. In the report to local managers, however, these results would be noted in summary form, and the fact that they were reported to executives would be indicated. Local managers, in turn, would then be able to include these findings in the feedback sessions with the employees they supervise. They could assure employees that their criticisms of a particular policy had been relayed to the top levels of management. (This statement allows local managers to concentrate on those findings for which they are responsible and on which they can act.) In most cases, the manager would also be able to point to recent policy changes resulting from previous surveys.

Monitoring the feedback process

Because the feedback process plays a key role in bringing about organizational change, its effectiveness should be monitored continuously. Depending on the nature of the survey program and the size of the organization, a number of monitoring techniques can be used. The survey administrator may observe survey feedback sessions or conduct them personally. On the other hand, both practices may be objected to if local managers are held responsible for survey feedback. Unless local managers assume this responsibility in these situations, they may seem too dependent on the survey administrator; their leadership role in the eyes of subordinates could be weakened.

In large organizations, it may be impractical for a survey administrator to observe or conduct feedback sessions. Mechanical systems, however, can be devised to monitor the process. The written record of the feedback session prepared by the local manager can be kept on file to give the regional survey administrator an idea of the content of each feedback session. In addition, each manager can describe the topics that were discussed, the actions (if any) that resulted, and the reactions of people at the meeting in a fairly detailed summary of each session. While this is not a foolproof system of monitoring, it does provide a written record that can be reviewed when conducting other surveys.

REFERENCES

Delbecq, A. L., Van de Ven, A. H., and Gustafson, D. H. *Group Techniques for Program Planning: A Guide to Nominal Group and Delphi Processes*, Scott, Foresman and Co., 1975.

Dodd, W. E. and Pesci, M. L. Managing morale through survey feedback. *Business Horizons,* June 1977, 36.

Edwards, A. L. *Techniques of Attitude Scale Construction,* Appleton Century Crofts, 1957.

Filley, A. C. *Interpersonal Conflict Resolution,* Scott, Foresman, 1975.

Guttman, L. The Basis for Scalagram Analysis. *American Sociological Review,* 1944, 9:139-50.

Suchman, E. The intensity component in scalagram analysis. In Stouffer, S. A. et al. *Measurement and Prediction,* Princeton University Press, 1950.

Torgerson, W. S. *Theory and Methods of Scaling,* Wiley, 1958.

A Final Word

Organizational surveys have many uses. Our observations have shown, however, that most organizations focus primarily on only one or two of the functions. Regardless of the primary reason for conducting a survey, organizations must take advantage of all its uses to maximize the effectiveness of the technique. Surveys should be used to provide management with information (feedback) about the organization that is not readily available through other means. This kind of data is valuable as an auditing tool, as a planning aid, and as a device for assessing organizational change. Surveys also help to predict or explain critical organizational events. They can act as a catalyst to stimulate communication and can provide a "safe" channel for upward communication. Organizational surveys can be effective training devices for managers; they offer the possibility of developing important skills and attaining valuable insights about the level of job satisfaction among employees. They can be used to evaluate the performance of the organization and to determine how well it meets employee needs. Finally, organizational surveys can provide the basis for the financial evaluation of employee attitudes.

Our biggest single disappointment in conducting surveys

is that most organizations do not consider using the technique until a serious problem occurs. Although surveys can be useful problem-solving tools, they can be much more valuable as preventive devices. A good systematic survey program often detects problems before they erupt. Thus, an ongoing survey program can serve to identify potential problems and to provide additional information on problems after they have been detected.

We have never seen a perfect survey, and you are not likely to have the first. We have, however, seen some very good surveys. The factors discussed in Chapter Four are intended to maximize the effectiveness of the survey. It is critical that the step-by-step process of survey design and administration be given careful attention. Careful attention to these standards will greatly increase your chances for success in survey work. Designing a poor survey is likely to lead to dysfunctional results and to diminish employees' trust and commitment. If you are not willing to conduct surveys properly, we advise against the use of the technique.

Survey programs can help to establish good management-worker relations and to improve organizational effectiveness. When used appropriately, a survey program can show workers that they are valued by the organization. When used inappropriately, a survey can be harmful. Executives and managers must be honest with employees about the intent of the survey. They must be responsive to the results and be willing to communicate findings and reactions to employees. Failure to do so is likely to jeopardize the utility of future surveys.

Surveys are effective, but they are not miraculous. They do not solve all problems, but they anticipate many. They have both instantaneous impact and lasting effects. If you decide to survey, prepare to learn bad as well as good things about your organization. If you conduct a survey, use the results! This can be hard work, but it is a very meaningful way to contribute to organizational health.

Appendix 1
A Guide to Nondirective Interviewing

Personal interviews with employees are an important part of the company's survey program. They supplement the survey questionnaire. Like the questionnaire, the interviews provide information about the attitudes, opinions, and feelings employees have toward their total work environment. However, information obtained from interviews is different from that obtained using questionnaires. Its content is usually more specific and often includes an explanation of the many conditions which may be contributing to or impeding the adequate functioning of an organization. With this combination of knowledge—the description of conditions provided by the questionnaire and the reasons behind the development of the conditions provided by the interviews—management is in a position to build on existing strengths and to direct constructive efforts at potential or existing problems.

The type of interviewing discussed here is known as the employee-centered approach. It is based on the idea that interviewers do not know in advance what the person being interviewed believes or feels. Interviewers should be interested in finding out how employees feel and what they think about those

128

aspects of their jobs which are important to them. Interviewers obtain this kind of information primarily by being listeners. They should also accept employee attitudes, feelings, and beliefs without judging their value or correctness.

This is somewhat different from your role as a manager. You, as an employee-centered interviewer will, in a sense, have to relinquish temporarily your usual mode of thinking and behavior and substitute for it a combination of characteristics and techniques unlike those you normally rely on to bring you success in dealing with your everyday responsibilities. The following discussion is intended to equip you with a working knowledge of the employee-centered interviewing technique.

Each interview has three segments: the beginning, the body, and the ending. Each of these segments has its own purposes and should be handled in a special way. This appendix describes the purposes and methods for each of these three phases of the interview.

THE BEGINNING OF THE INTERVIEW

Purpose To start employees talking by
   a) putting them at ease. Interviewers accomplish this primarily by being friendly, interested, and sincere.
   b) assuring them that what they say will be kept strictly confidential.
   c) defining their role for them. That is, interviewers tell them that the interview is being held so that they can talk about whatever is important to them in their jobs.

Method A standard introduction

The standard introduction

Some people come into a survey interview situation feeling a little tense and uneasy. It may be the first time they've participated in an interview program, and they may not know just what to expect—or what will be expected of them. The purpose of the standard introduction is to relieve whatever uncertainty and uneasiness employees have by orienting them to the interview.

On an intellectual level, the standard introduction is an attempt to inform employees what the interview is all about. Employees are told who the interviewer is, what is appropriate subject matter, and what ground rules the interview will follow. On an emotional level, the standard introduction is aimed at alleviating any anxiety that employees may be experiencing because they have been thrown into this situation—one which may be unfamiliar and consequently, somewhat threatening. Relieving this kind of anxiety can be done in a variety of ways, but the quickest way to put someone at ease is to display genuine friendliness. That is, interviewers should greet employees warmly, invite them to sit down and get comfortable, and accept their handshake, if they offer it. Additionally, interviewers should present the introduction in a way that indicates that they are interested in helping employees understand what this whole process is all about. Despite the fact that the interviewer has to repeat the introduction many times to many people, it is the sole time that individual employees hear it, and they deserve to have it presented in a way that will have meaning for them.

These seemingly simple gestures serve to allay tension because they indicate to employees that they are recognized as people whose opinions and attitudes have value and will be accepted for their own sake. These gestures also encourage employees to accept interviewers for what they are—representatives of the company who are sincerely interested in hearing employees discuss various feelings and attitudes about their jobs.

Begin each interview with any of the following three variations of a standard introduction:

> "I am _____ from _____. Did you fill out the questionnaire that was given here a while back? Well, that was the first part of the survey. The second part is this interview.
>
> "I want to assure you that our interview will be completely confidential. When all the interviews are completed, we will analyze all of the opinions and attitudes

that we have received, and this will give us a general overall picture of the morale in this unit.

"Now, I don't have any questions to ask, or anything I'd like to talk about. We'll talk about only those things that you yourself want to discuss.

"I'm _____ from the personnel department. As you probably were told, the questionnaire that was given here recently was the first part of a survey that's being conducted and this interview is the second part. The interview is really all yours and I'm interested in anything you would like to talk about. I don't have many questions to ask, and I will be happy to listen to anything you care to discuss. I want to assure you that whatever you say is strictly confidential. I'm not interested in identifying you personally. I merely add up all the comments I receive and make my report on the group as a whole."

"My name is _____ from the _____ department. Did you have an opportunity to fill out the questionnaire they gave here? The interviewing which started Monday is the second part of the survey. In this interview today, I hope you will feel free to talk about anything you might like to discuss. I'm not going to quote you personally, but I do add up all the opinions I hear from people and summarize them when I have completed interviewing in any one department."

Keep in mind the following two rules when making the introduction:

1) Although the introduction should be memorized, it should be spoken in a very conversational manner.
2) Only those things illustrated in the examples are to be part of the introduction. Any elaboration is completely inappropriate.

If it is presented in a friendly and sincere way, the introduction will put the employees at ease and give them the impression that what they have to say is important. After the introduction, employees usually begin talking.

Expanding or modifying the standard introduction

The standard introduction doesn't work • Even after a well-presented introduction, some employees do not start talking. Frequently, this happens because they still do not know where to begin or what to say. They may even indicate this very candidly, by saying something like this:

> "Well, I've never had an interview like this, and I just don't know what to say."

or

> "Is there anything in particular you want me to talk about?"

Such statements may "throw" new interviewers if they are not ready for them. When talking to employees who do not respond to the introduction, be sure to avoid citing specific topics. Some inexperienced interviewers tend to answer, "Well, talk about your work, your boss, and things like that." Such a comment could easily have the effect of setting limitations on what employees talk about since it could be construed as a list of the only subjects that they are expected to discuss.

There are several ways to encourage employees who are not reassured adequately by the introduction to start talking. For example, interviewers can say, "Well, why don't you tell me how things generally are going for you here." Or, if employees appear very reluctant to begin talking, interviewers can say, "Tell me how you happened to come to this company."

If these kinds of comments fail to evoke a response, it may be necessary to work with employees for a while, since they may still be nervous or apprehensive. In such situations, it is usually worthwhile to talk about the weather, current events, or some topic completely unrelated to the work situation. This usually helps set employees at ease by allowing them to see that interviewers are not people to be afraid of, but people who are there to listen uncritically to anything they have to say. After interviewers have helped employees to become sufficiently relaxed, they can say something like this: "I wonder if you'd care to tell me how things are going for you on your job and how you feel about working here." Such a comment usually prompts employees to start talking.

The interviewer knows the employee • Occasionally, an old friend, a casual acquaintance, or a former co-worker is among a group of people to be interviewed. Whenever this happens, it is important to give such an individual the option of talking to another team member. People may feel uncomfortable or "put on the spot" during the course of a survey interview regardless of who interviews them. Part of this is due to the fact that employees are being asked to express their real feelings. And very few people are inclined to speak their minds without some reasons to believe that what they say will not be used against them. Such a guarantee is partly provided by the anonymity of the employee-centered interview.

However, when interviewers know employees personally, employees may be somewhat reluctant to reveal their feelings candidly. Consequently, interviewers in this situation should ascertain how employees really feel about being interviewed by someone they know. If it appears that the effectiveness of the interview will be impaired, interviewers should encourage employees to talk to someone else on the survey team, as demonstrated in the following example.

(The interviewer has just finished the standard introduction.)

Emp: Say, Ms. Becker, I think we've met before. I helped you process all those personnel files.

Int: I thought your face looked familiar. Since we've already met, this interview can't really be anonymous. While I can assure you it will be completely confidential, you may prefer to talk to one of the other interviewers. I certainly would have no objections to your doing that.

Emp: Oh no, it doesn't bother me any. I'd just as soon talk to you.

Int: Well, in that case, how are things going?

The employee has no prior knowledge of the survey • Typically, the interview portion of the survey program follows the administration of the questionnaire. As a result, employees have a fairly good idea of what the survey is all about by the time they are interviewed because the administration of the questionnaire includes a brief description of the purpose and methods of the survey program. This explanation usually establishes the appropriate framework within which the interview will be conducted. When it is coupled with the standard introduction, employees have enough information about the survey to make their participation meaningful.

Employees who have not attended the administration meeting, however, may not know what is going on. This is especially true for the members of a group who are interviewed first since they do not have the benefit of the usual information passed through the grapevine. Interviewers who encounter one of these employees should explain what the survey is all about. Even if the words in the introduction are familiar, the concept and goals of the survey may not be. Interviewers should remember not to speed through or gloss over explanations. Rather, they should remember that they may be talking about something completely new to some employees. Therefore, they should explain the survey in a way that enlists employees' cooperation and active participation. The following example demonstrates one successful way of handling this situation.

Int: Won't you come in and sit down?

Emp: Thank you.

Int: I'm Sue Becker. Did you fill out one of our questionnaires?

Emp: No, I didn't. I wasn't here that week because I had to take some time off.

Int: Oh, I see. Probably you've heard about the survey. Perhaps I can tell you how the program works. There are two parts to the program. First of all, the questionnaire contains general questions covering various things about your job. In addition to that questionnaire, we also conduct these interviews, which give you an opportunity to talk about your job in your own words in a strictly confidential manner.

I have no questions to ask or anything in particular I'd like you to talk about. Rather, I'm just interested in anything you'd care to discuss.

Emp: Oh, I see.

Int: None of the things you say in the interview will be discussed with management. When all of the interviews are completed, we'll analyze all of the opinions and attitudes expressed, and this will give us a general picture of morale in your unit.

Interviewing supervisors • Supervisory personnel are usually interviewed as a separate group. Occasionally, however, they are interviewed as part of the unit they supervise. Whenever this occurs, supervisors should be interviewed first, and the standard introduction should be modified along the following lines:

Int: Hi, I'm Sue Becker. Since I've been assigned to interview in your department, I thought I'd talk to you first and give you a brief description about how we go about this portion of the survey. First of all, we don't ask employees any questions; as a matter of fact, we assure them they can discuss anything they wish. The only time we do any talking is to encourage them to talk or get clarification on something they've mentioned. After the interviews in any one group are finished, we write a report describing the overall conditions and feelings in the unit.
Before I start talking to your people, I wonder if you could tell me a little bit about the department—I'd be interested in anything you'd care to say.

After this modification of the introduction, the rest of the interview with supervisors should be conducted exactly as it is with other employees.

The employee interrupts the introduction • In addition to its other goals, the standard introduction tries to get employees to start talking. If they interrupt the introduction by discussing what is on their minds, interviewers should just dispense with any opening remarks. There is no need to bring an interview which is already underway back to its starting point. If employees need little or no encouragement and reassurance to begin the interview, accept the situation for what it is and concentrate on keeping them talking.

The employee has no complaints • Occasionally, employees respond to the introduction by saying, "I have no complaints; I'm very happy" (meaning that they have nothing to say or nothing to add to the survey), and stop right there. Needless to say, these employees probably need a little encouragement— some explanation and reassurance about the nature of the survey. Any efforts along this line will be worthwhile, for you can be fairly certain that almost all employees have something to contribute to the pool of attitudes and opinions being gathered. In such cases, never dismiss employees or take their word that there is no point in continuing the interview. A comment of this kind may be an indication of a kind of refusal to participate in the survey, or employees may feel that anything they might say would be inappropriate for an interview. In either case, interviewers can say something like this:

> *Int:*   Well, I wonder if you'd give me a little bit of a rundown on how you feel about your job. What are some of the things which cause you to feel good about it? Maybe you can also give me some idea how things are going for you.

As the above example shows, interviewers' comments can encourage employees to make comments about their jobs. Once employees start talking, other employee-centered techniques can be used to keep them talking.

THE BODY OF THE INTERVIEW

Purposes   1) To encourage employees to talk about their feelings, attitudes, and opinions about their jobs
2) To help them express their thoughts fully and clearly
3) To explore the solutions that employees propose to organizational problems

Methods   1) The use of behavioral stimulation
a) listening
b) nodding the head
c) smiling

2) The use of verbal stimulation
   a) acceptance statements
   b) repetitive statements
   c) probing statements
   d) interpretive statements
3) The use of the pause

Behavioral stimulation

The interviewer's own actions and behavior can encourage employees to express attitudes, ideas and feelings.

Obvious listening • Most people want what they say taken seriously. Consequently, in successfully conducted employee-centered interviews, interviewers should communicate their interest in what employees are saying. One of the ways to do this is simply to pay attention. Employees who perceive that their comments are holding the attention of the interviewer—that, in fact, the interviewer looks sincerely interested—will be prompted to freely express their thoughts.

Looking sincerely interested is difficult when you don't feel this way. Consequently, you must actually intend to listen to what employees are trying to communicate in order to convince them that you are sincere. This is not always easy. After several interviews, the same topics may begin to appear in employees' comments. It would be a mistake, however, to take the attitude, "Oh, I've heard this before—no need to really pay attention," because you never really know whether you have heard it or not. After all, some employees may present a new viewpoint; they may see a subject from different vantage points than other people who have mentioned it. Therefore, you should assume an almost naive attitude toward each interview—as though you were hearing everything for the first time. In many cases, you will find that this is true.

Employees should be allowed to talk without being interrupted. Interviewers can communicate their willingness to listen by letting employees speak without constantly interrupting them. Even if employees' comments seem to need explanation or clarification, interviewers should wait for employees to finish talking about a topic before asking questions. It is important to remember that interviewers who generally appear inattentive or uninterested alienate employees. Such alienation frequently contributes to the breakdown of the interview.

The nod and the smile • By displaying genuine interest
in what is being said, interviewers can establish a basic rapport
with employees and encourage them to speak freely. Such encouragement, however, has to be given periodically throughout
the interview. By nodding their heads whenever an idea is expressed interviewers indicate to the individual that they have
been listening—that they understand and accept the employee's
comments.

By the same token, a smile from interviewers now and
then is also reassuring to employees. It is an indication that interviewers are sympathetic toward employees and wish to give them
moral support. Such a smile also conveys an interviewer's willingness to accept whatever employees choose to say.

Verbal stimulation

Because some employees are inclined to talk freely, their
interviews proceed smoothly, with only occasional behavioral
stimulation (obvious listening, smiling, and nodding) needed
from interviewers. In most cases, however, verbal stimulation
should supplement behavioral stimulation. Verbal stimulation is
the use of statements to keep employees talking. These are statements that accept, repeat, probe, or interpret employees' comments.

Showing acceptance • The following statements indicate
to employees that the interviewer understands what has been
said. These statements can be spoken either while employees are
talking or after they complete an idea. They include comments
such as "Um-hum," or "That's interesting," or "I see." The use of
such statements accomplishes two ends. First, it shows
employees that the interviewer is listening and accepts what has
been said. Second, it keeps the interview moving along by encouraging the individual to keep talking.

The repeat • The *repeat* is probably the most frequently
used verbal stimulation technique in employee-centered interviewing. With this technique, the interviewer repeats the exact
meaning of the employee's words in a slightly questioning tone.
The repeat can be used in many situations, but it is particularly
helpful when the employee a) shows strong feelings toward a

subject but appears somewhat reluctant to discuss it; b) "rambles" about subjects unrelated to the work situation; or c) asks what other people have said in their interviews.

The employee shows strong feeling toward a subject. Employees sometimes mention topics and then drop them. Interviewers can encourage elaboration of these feelings by using the repeat. That is, after a very brief pause, interviewers repeat the employees' own words to them (or the exact meaning of their words) with a slightly questioning but nonjudgmental tone.

Caution   When using the repeat, do not misquote employees. For example, if an employee says, "They should do a better job of handling pay here," be certain not to misquote by saying, "You say they don't pay well here?" Misquoting can sound like an accusation or like an interviewer's rejection of the problem. If this happens, whatever rapport has been established may be nullified, and employees may be unwilling to say anything more, simply because they will no longer feel that they have a receptive audience.

The employee rambles. The interviewer may also use the repeat with employees who ramble. There are many reasons why people ramble when they talk. Among them are the following:

They do not know what to say. Some employees don't know how to start so they say the first thing that comes to mind and just continue with it.

They want to test the interviewer. Some people do not wish to discuss pertinent material until they are certain that the interviewer is a person they can trust. So they just continue throwing out comments to see how the interviewer will react to them.

They are afraid. Some employees wish to avoid talking about their work situation because they fear that they will put their jobs in jeopardy by speaking freely. Instead, they may talk about a number of subjects which are completely unrelated to their work.

They may want to impress the interviewer. Feeling somewhat threatened by the interview situation, they

may need to bolster their self-esteem. These people keep
talking in an attempt to prove to the interviewer that they
too share in the control of the interview situation.
They may just be talkative people.

When employees ramble, listen very carefully. In most
cases, through the use of the repeat you will be able to focus their
attention on pertinent subjects which come up in their comments.

> *Emp:* . . . and I came to work here about three years ago.
> I've worked at a number of places but this is proba-
> bly the best, I always get along with everybody and
> I like all kinds of work. I've done just about every-
> thing there is to do from driving a school bus to
> janitoring to selling, and as I say, I like them all.
>
> *Int:* I think I understand how you feel. You mentioned
> that you like all kinds of work but this is probably
> the best?
>
> *Emp:* Oh yes, it's more steady, the working conditions
> are better and it's cleaner.

In the above example, the employee rambles on and on
but does make a remark about his or her present work. The interviewer waits until the employee pauses and then repeats the
comment in a mildly questioning manner. This repeat usually
brings employees back to discussing their job situation.
    The employee asks what other people have said in their
interviews. Occasionally, employees question interviewers about
the comments which co-workers have made. Sometimes this is
merely a way of trying to get interviewers to assure them that
they are not making inappropriate remarks. Or, employees may
merely want to test interviewers to see whether the results of the
survey are really confidential. On the other hand, they may only
be making idle conversation. In the following example, the interviewer reassures the employee that survey results are confidential but also directs the discussion back to those things that are
important to the worker and relevant to the job situation.

> *Emp:* . . . but our division needs to be reorganized. Mr.
> Werner isn't very efficient, although he does work
> hard. Haven't some of the others told you that?

Int: I can understand why you'd want to know what the other employees have said, but as you know, these interviews are confidential and I really can't discuss them with you.

Emp: Oh yes, I guess that's right.

Int: (Pause) You were saying that although Mr. Werner works very hard, he's not very efficient. Could you tell me a little bit more about that.

Emp: Well, mainly I meant the way he never seems to plan anything. Most of the time he makes a decision about what he wants or how he wants it done at the last minute. We never have time to get ready for anything.

The repeat doesn't work. As you are well aware, no technique is foolproof. Occasionally, the use of the repeat may backfire. Whenever this occurs, it is important to try again, as the following example illustrates.

Emp: . . . had the store just about one year so they've given us very nice working conditions.

Int: Um-hum.

Emp: This store pays as good as any place in town, but this area has a very low salary scale.

Int: You say the store pays as good as any place in town, but that the area has a low salary scale?

Emp: Well, that's what I said.

Int: I'd be interested in your reasons for feeling this way.

Emp: Well, I think it's because it's a resort town and lots of people . . . .

The probing statement • This technique is especially effective in dealing with two kinds of situations—when employees' comments are incomplete and when employees attempt to evade their role (doing the talking) by asking the interviewer questions. In these situations employees may

generalize so that their statements have limited meaning
express contradictory opinions
merely mention a topic, without giving any details

fail to identify the people they are talking about
question the value of the survey
ask if employees will be informed about the results of the
survey
question the interviewer about the company policy or
procedures
try to interview the interviewer
ask about the confidential nature of the survey
ask the interviewer for advice

The employee generalizes. Employees are often unaware
that their comments may be completely new to the interviewer.
As a result, they may refer to things in a very obscure way and
only touch on very important points. Whenever this occurs, it is
the interviewer's responsibility to use any of the techniques
available to obtain specific information which will help clarify
employees' remarks.

> *Emp:* . . . we had a Division Manager come in. He was
> new and during the first few days changes were
> really made. You should see how they affected the
> group. In my years here I've had several changes
> like that, but never with such an effect.
>
> *Int:* I see. You say that during the first few days some
> changes were made?
>
> *Emp:* They sure were. Things were really tough.
>
> *Int:* Could you tell me about some of the changes which
> took place?
>
> *Emp:* Well, there were a lot of them. First of all, he re-
> scheduled all of the passes and lunch hours and if
> that wasn't enough he . . . .

In this example, the employee states that changes were
made which affected the work group. It is important for the interviewer to know what the changes were. In order to obtain this
information, the interviewer uses the repeat and follows it up
with a probing question. The combination of these two
techniques prompts the employee to clarify the initial statement.

The employee makes contradictory statements. Sometimes employees make apparently contradictory statements.
Whenever this happens, the interviewer should encourage

employees to discuss the comments that need clarification. The following example demonstrates how this might be done.

> *Emp:* We've been so busy in our department that I even forget to take my pass sometimes. But I really like to work here because I feel no one is particularly pushing me to get things done. Sometimes, though, you have to hunt for work and things to do when the big bosses walk through because we've been told to look busy.
>
> *Int:* You say that you are so busy in your department that you sometimes forget to take your pass. Then later, I think you stated that you sometimes have to hunt for work and things to do. Did I understand you correctly?
>
> *Emp:* That's right. When the mail comes in we have to break our backs, but then other times we worry that someone will come in and see us when there's a lull in the mail.

In obtaining an accurate picture of such a situation, the interviewer should not risk antagonizing employees by appearing to challenge them. Rather, they should repeat the comments in a way that makes employees aware of the discrepancy. If interviewers can convey the impression that they are asking questions not because they doubt the accuracy of what employees have said but because they want to clarify the statements, employees usually begin to discuss their statements more fully, thereby clearing up whatever seemed contradictory.

The employee merely mentions a problem. Occasionally, employees mention a problem but give no further information about it. In such cases, the interviewer should encourage them to bring out any details which might help to explain their attitudes and feelings. The kind of probing used in the following example is usually sufficient to encourage employees to discuss the subject in greater detail.

> *Emp:* There are a lot of conflicting rumors around here. One day you hear one thing and the next day the opposite, so we need to know more about things.
>
> *Int:* Would you care to tell me more about that?

> *Emp:* Well, just last week there was a rumor that they were going to close this plant. This doesn't make much sense because we all know business has been good, but it still shook us up.

<u>The employee is uncertain about identifying people by name.</u> Some employees misinterpret the confidential nature of the interview. They believe that they should refrain from using any names in interviews because they are not identified by name in survey reports. This can present a problem since it causes employees to talk in a somewhat roundabout fashion. The following example shows how to deal with situations of this kind.

> *Emp:* Some of the people could really use some lessons in—what do you call it—public relations. You know, they could treat people more politely.
>
> *Int:* You feel that some of the people could be more considerate.
>
> *Emp:* I sure do.
>
> *Int:* I'd be interested in knowing why you feel this way.
>
> *Emp:* Well, he's always shouting at people. He never thinks to take someone aside and talk to him.
>
> *Int:* You say he's always shouting at people.
>
> *Emp:* That's right. Well, the Manager, Mr. . . . I—uh—can we use names? I didn't think we were supposed to.
>
> *Int:* Well, I'm interested in knowing how you feel and it certainly would help me understand the situation. You can use names and anything else that will help you tell your story. Again, though, I want to assure you that anything you say is confidential.
>
> *Emp:* Well, Mr. Wright, he's our personnel manager . . . .

In this example, the interviewer is interested in learning the identity of the person who is "always shouting at people." He or she also wants to explain that the purpose of the interview is to get a complete picture of how the employee feels. So, along with the encouragement to speak freely ("naming names," if that will add to the comments), the employee should also be reassured about the confidential nature of the interview. These reassurances usually prompt the employee to discuss his or her feelings more fully and explicitly.

The employee questions the value of the survey. Employees may ask about the purposes of the survey. In some cases, such a question is used as a defense or as a challenge because the employee is anxious and uncomfortable in the interview. Regardless of the motivation for such questions, interviewers should only use them to elicit further discussion of employee attitudes and opinions.

> *Emp:* Do you think this survey will do any good?
>
> *Int:* Well, after we have interviewed everyone in this department, a report of the findings is sent to management here. After this, a report will be made to your group and at that time if there are any problems you'll hear about what will be done to improve them. Since you brought it up, is there anything you think the survey should do?

As you can see, the interviewer explains what will be done with the survey results without in any way making promises or committing the management of the unit to any action. More importantly, however, the interviewer uses the employee's question to accomplish the goal of the interview, that is, to get as much information as possible about how the person feels and thinks about the various aspects of his or her job.

Employees ask whether they will be informed of the survey results. People usually want to know the outcome of any venture in which they've participated. Consequently, it's not unusual for employees to ask whether they will hear about the results of the survey. They may also be challenging the interviewer with this kind of a question because this is the best defense in a threatening situation. The following example suggests how to handle these situations.

> *Emp:* Tell me, will we ever hear about the results or is this just one of those things that you do and then never hear about again?
>
> *Int:* Well, as I mentioned, we make our report of the overall findings to your manager. After he's had a

>*Emp:* chance to read it over and digest it, he in turn will
> report back the results to all of you.
>
> *Emp:* I see.
>
> *Int:* Do you mind telling me how things are going for
> you these days?
>
> *Emp:* Well, not too bad, I suppose. There are a couple of
> things . . . .

The employee asks questions about policy and proce-dures. Employees may ask very direct questions about their compensation or their status in the organization. Interviewers should not answer these questions. Instead, they should make employees' problems the subject of discussion again by asking them whether they have discussed the matter with management.

> *Emp:* You know there is something that's been bugging
> me for quite a while. You work in personnel, maybe
> you can tell me if it's true that the company won't
> allow you to take three weeks of vacation at one
> time.
>
> *Int:* You're wondering what the company policy is on
> this matter. Have you talked to anyone here about
> this?
>
> *Emp:* Oh no. I've never brought it up.
>
> *Int:* You've never mentioned it to anyone?
>
> *Emp:* I've been meaning to talk to the manager, but every
> time I try to see him his door is closed.

The employee tries to interview the interviewer. Occasionally, an employee attempts to discuss the interviewer. As soon as the interviewer becomes aware that the employee is trying to reverse their roles, he or she should return the discussion to the employee and the work situation.

> *Emp:* How long have you been at this company?
>
> *Int:* Eight years.
>
> *Emp:* You must have a very interesting job. How do you
> like it?
>
> *Int:* I enjoy it very much. You mentioned earlier that
> your job was interesting. Could you tell me about
> those things which make it interesting for you?

The employee questions the confidentiality of the survey.
Some employees do not understand how survey data is used. For
example, they may fear that what they say will be reported to
their superiors. So, when employees ask, "Is this interview really
confidential?" they may be requesting an assurance that their
jobs will be protected if they express their thoughts. Interviewers
should respond with a reply like this:

> I certainly can assure you that it is. What we do is
> this—when the survey is completed, we analyze all the
> results and summarize them in a general overall report
> for the group as a whole—but in no case are the remarks
> of any employee ever reported or pinpointed.

The employee asks the interviewer for advice. Employees
may ask the interviewer for direction or guidance. Whenever this
happens, it is important to remember that survey interviews are
not intended to be counseling sessions. As a matter of fact, to give
advice to employees may do them and the survey program a disservice. Because employees see you as a representative of management, they are likely to take whatever you say quite seriously.
As a result, even though you might be speaking quite generally,
employees might feel that any suggestions you make should be
followed. Employees might later cite your advice as authority for
their actions. This puts employees in the position of taking action
or making a decision on the advice of someone who is quite removed from the situation—someone who has no formal responsibility for employees, who may not have all the facts, and who
probably will not even be on the scene when the matter is handled. The following conversation shows how to turn an
employee's request for advice to the interviewer's advantage.

> *Emp:* Well, anyway, we're always running out of stock or
>   else the merchandise isn't where we can get at it
>   easily. Mr. Kane, our store manager, came down
>   here the other day and he asked me why there
>   weren't more socks on the counter. I really had no
>   idea of what to say. I sure didn't want to say that
>   the way my boss, Mr. Smart, orders merchandise
>   leaves something to be desired, but, gee, I didn't
>   feel I should be chewed out either.

Int: So, the upshot was you really felt on the spot?

Emp: Yes, I did. Luckily for me a customer walked up and asked me a question. So I excused myself and took care of the sale. By the time I finished, Mr. Kane had left.

Int: Um-hum.

Emp: Do you think the next time I see Mr. Kane I should talk to him about the matter since he brought it up in the first place?

Int: I really think you're in a better position than I am to answer that. What do you think is the best way to handle it?

Emp: Well, I'm not sure. If Mr. Smart didn't work so hard and wasn't so pleasant with us, it would be awfully hard to work here, but on the other hand . . . .

Interpreting the employee's comments • It is not always easy for people to express their feelings and ideas clearly. Often, they can only describe their feelings in general terms. When they are put in the position of trying to describe and explain these feelings to a second party, they have difficulty being specific. For example, employees may express dissatisfaction about their relationships with co-workers. However, they may only be able to describe the problem in a very roundabout way. Perhaps they have never really thought through the matter that they are discussing. If interviewers have a firm grasp of the ideas that employees are struggling to communicate, they can clarify them by making remarks that attempt to synthesize the employees' comments.

Suggesting that the interviewer try to help employees crystallize their thoughts and feelings does not mean that the interviewer should put words into employees' mouths. It merely means that the interviewer can help employees clarify their own thoughts and feelings. The following example shows how this can be done.

Emp: Well, the girl that I work with has been here—just like me—about six months. She told me, right when she started, that she's only interested in this job until she gets married in June. She stays on a

> break . . . sometimes half an hour, she doesn't care. And nobody says anything to her about it. She hardly ever helps with stock and then last week she got the same raise I did.
>
> *Int:* Um-hum.
>
> *Emp:* It just seems that hard work doesn't pay off. . . . It isn't appreciated. It doesn't seem right, does it?
>
> *Int:* Your raise seems to have little meaning to you. . . . As a result, you actually seem a little discouraged.
>
> *Emp:* That's right. I thought my raise meant that they felt I was doing a good job. But she got the same raise . . . really for doing nothing. It just doesn't seem worth the effort.

The pause

Employees may stop talking even if the interview is underway and if an appropriate atmosphere has been established for it. Whenever this happens, interviewers should not be too eager to fill the conversational void. Instead, they should allow the silence to continue for a while to see if employees will begin talking again. This often happens. When the interview has been running smoothly, employees may pause to summon their courage or to collect their thoughts before plunging into another topic. Or, they may have finished talking about one subject and may not quite know what to say next. Interviewers should wait in a relaxed manner for employees to break the silence. Silence on the part of employees may be somewhat unsettling, especially to new interviewers. Accustomed to social situations in which people talk most of the time, interviewers may tend to break the silence too soon instead of waiting for employees to do it.

Of course, the silence can continue too long. When that happens, interviewers can repeat the employee's last statement or a point that they wish to have clarified and then say:

"Would you care to discuss this topic further?"

or

"Is there anything else you'd like to talk about?"

Exploring solutions expected by employees

Since surveys are conducted to improve organizational effectiveness and job satisfaction, it is often advisable to explore employees' suggestions for improvements. This can be done in several different ways. For example, if employees mention a problem, interviewers can ask any of the following questions:

"What do you think could be done to improve that situation?"

"Do you have a suggestion as to how this might be remedied?"

"If it were up to you, how would you go about handling that?"

"I wonder if you have any thoughts on how this situation could be corrected (solved, improved, changed, etc.)?"

When employees focus on one specific problem, such as the length of time since the last pay increase, interviewers can say,

"I gather from your comments that a raise would resolve your whole problem."

or

"It appears that a raise would change your whole outlook on things."

These questions are not to be used routinely or mechanically; they should be used only to arrive at a representative sample of employee opinion about the corrective action that they would like to see take place.

Employees do not always know the solutions to their problems. At the same time, the fact that employees may have no suggestions is worth knowing because in such cases, any actions that management takes will not encounter employees' resistance or appear unresponsive to employee needs. When employees do have well-formed solutions and expectations, however, they should describe them as fully as possible since any management actions that are consistent with these suggestions may be especially successful while those that run counter to them are likely to fail. Thus, in either case, knowledge of employee expectations can be extremely valuable.

Exploring employee solutions to problems serves a number of other useful purposes. Merely posing the question of possible solutions can help employees develop a certain degree of insight and can encourage them to analyze their feelings in greater depth. This kind of inner searching can also help interviewers obtain a better understanding of an organization's impact on employees.

Asking employees for possible solutions also acts as a triggering device because it often gets employees to think of other aspects of problems that may not have been mentioned. In addition, it forces employees to confront the problems that managers face when they attempt to take corrective action. This realization may improve the relationship between managers and employees and can help bring about desired changes.

The success of this technique depends upon the interviewer's ability to use it appropriately. The following hints may be helpful.

1) The technique should not be used in response to every problem mentioned in interviews. It should be used only when interviewers think that it will serve one or more of the purposes described above.

2) Interviewers should not ask these questions in a challenging or threatening way. Their tone of voice should convey a sincere interest in exploring all possible solutions to employees' problems.

Caution   Interviewers should never leave employees with the idea that the problem will be corrected or resolved in the manner that employees suggest. Interviewers are never in a position to make or even imply such a commitment.

THE END OF THE INTERVIEW

Most interviews end naturally. However, interviewers should realize that the end is approaching when employees a) start repeating previous statements; b) make comments like this:

"I guess that's about it"; or c) move toward the edge of the chair or start to stand up.

It is the interviewer's responsibility to bring the interview to a close when employees seem to have nothing more to say. For example, the interviewer can summarize what has been said and ask, "Does that sum it up?" or "Is there anything else you would like to add?" If employees indicate that they have nothing more to say, the interviewer can conclude the interview like this: "Well, if there isn't anything else you'd like to talk about, thank you very much. It was nice talking with you."

Caution   Interviews can be terminated too rapidly. Sometimes employees must work up to what they want to say. Therefore, interviewers should use all the techniques at their disposal to insure that employees express everything on their minds.

Appendix II
Instructions for Survey Administration

You have been asked to come to this meeting today to participate in an attitude survey by filling out a questionnaire. Since it is important that people in each group taking the questionnaire receive the same instructions, I would like to read them to you. I want you to know that our company considers this survey very important, and I hope you will give your full cooperation by being completely frank in filling it out.

As many of you know, the company is administering attitude surveys. These surveys are for the purpose of finding out how you feel about the company and the many other things connected with your job. The company is interested in your opinions about the things that you like and the things that you believe should be changed or improved.

No one in our unit will ever see your individual answers, so please feel free to express yourself frankly. All of the information obtained in this questionnaire will be compiled and analyzed in terms of broad employee groups within our unit. In that way no individual's responses can be identified. So again, let me assure you on behalf of the company that all the information obtained in this questionnaire will be strictly confidential. As soon as possible, we will receive a report of the findings and after I have had an opportunity to study and digest the results, they will then be passed on to you.

Before we discuss how to fill out the questionnaire, you are asked to supply some additional information. This information, like your answers to the questionnaire itself, will be kept completely confidential. Since this survey is being conducted throughout the company, the information gathered will make it possible for the company to better understand how men and women in both full-time and part-time jobs feel about their work. If you will open the booklet to page 1 you will find this information located on the right-hand side of the page *(show booklet)*.

(At this point the manager explains how questions asking for demographic information and job activities should be answered.)

Now please look at the pages that have the words *YOUR COMMENTS,* printed at the top.

After you have completed the questionnaire, please make any comments on these pages that you feel will add meaning to the survey. I strongly urge you to write any comments you choose because we would like this survey to be as complete and meaningful as possible.

Before you begin filling out the questionnaire, there are a few additional comments I'd like to make. Remember to read the questions carefully, but do not spend a great deal of time on any one item. In surveys of this kind, your first reaction to a question is usually best. Be certain not to skip any questions or pages. In marking your answers, make your marks black and heavy. When you have answered all the questions in the questionnaire, write your comments on the comments pages. When you have completed your comments, make sure the front of the questionnaire is the cover page, and place your booklet in the envelope provided and seal it. As you leave the room, put your envelope in this box. I would like to appoint ＿＿＿＿＿＿ and ＿＿＿＿＿ to personally
                              (name)   *(name)*
handle the mailing of these booklets to the center. You will find the mailing instructions and the materials you will need on that table.

Does anyone have any questions at all? (Allow time for questions).

All right, please begin.

Appendix III

Validation of the Index of Organizational Reactions with the JDI, the MSQ, and the Faces Scales

Job satisfaction has been of great interest to individuals, organizations, and even entire social systems for many years.[1] It is generally believed that the study of job satisfaction should be able to contribute to the theory and application of motivation, attitudes, behaviors, and preferences within organizations (Smith, 1957). Researchers have conducted studies utilizing job satisfaction measures as both dependent and independent variables of theoretical and applied importance. Organizations have systematically examined measures of job satisfaction as organizationally relevant outcomes and as sources of other important outcomes. Thousands of such studies have been conducted or supported by governmental agencies.

The basis of all empirical study of job satisfaction is the

1. *A revised version of an article by Dunham, Smith, and Blackburn from the Academy of Management Journal, 1977, 20:420-32.*

instrument used to assess the affective responses. In recent years, a number of instruments for measuring job satisfaction have appeared (e.g., Faces Scales, Job Descriptive Index, Minnesota Satisfaction Questionnaire, etc.). "Unfortunately, little research has been performed comparing standardized satisfaction measures" (Gillett and Schwab, 1975, p. 313).

Smith, Kendall, and Hulin (1969) have stated that good measures of job satisfaction should: (1) separate the various aspects of satisfaction from one another; (2) agree with other, equivalent measures; (3) be useful with a wide range of persons from a wide range of jobs and a variety of situations; (4) be intuitively understandable; (5) be short; (6) allow group administrations; and (7) require low expenditures of time and money.

The major objective of the present study was to investigate the validity of the Index of Organizational Reactions (IOR) (Smith, 1962; 1976). The IOR consists of eight scales containing a total of forty-two items. It has been used as the core of twelve different questionnaires and has been used in several thousand locations among distinctly different work functions within a single large organization. . . .

A two-phase validity study was undertaken. In phase I, the factor analytic structure of the IOR scales was examined across several samples and over time. Factor analysis is a statistical technique which allows an examination of the eight facets of satisfaction tapped by the forty-two IOR items. The results indicate whether or not the forty-two items group together into the eight facets as intended. In phase II, the IOR was placed into a multitrait-multimethod matrix (Campbell and Fiske, 1959) with a set of Faces Scales (Kunin, 1955; Dunham and Herman, 1975), the Job Descriptive Index (JDI) (Smith, et al., 1969), and the Minnesota Satisfaction Questionnaire (MSQ) (Weiss, Dawis, England, and Lofquist, 1967) to investigate convergent and discriminant validities for all four methods of measuring job satisfaction. . . . This technique is used to determine whether the various methods of measuring satisfaction are all measuring the same constructs (satisfaction facets). It also helps to determine whether it is possible to discriminate between the various satisfaction facets—that is, whether separate facets can actually be measured. In addition, the four methods were examined for validity differences as a function of sex and type of job held by the respondent (operative versus supervisory).

PHASE I: FACTOR ANALYTIC STUDIES

Method

Subjects • Five samples were drawn from several branches of one organization (Sears, Roebuck and Company), and data were collected over a three-year period. The samples were selected to include workers from a wide range of jobs and a variety of situations. The researchers chose from a quarter of a mil-

TABLE 1   Sample Characteristics.

Characteristics/Sample[a]	II	III	IV	V
Age				
< 30	157	657	748	748
30-40	146	1857	1096	1375
41-55	263	1525	1116	1196
> 55	86	354	226	260
Sex				
Male	319	3975	2536	2715
Female	322	392	636	817
Education				
Some H.S.	89	89	NA[b]	21
H.S. grad.	417	1352	NA	472
2 yrs. college	70	624	NA	363
3 yrs. college	19	250	NA	164
College grad.	26	1642	NA	1665
Some grad. tr.	15	281	NA	427
Adv. degree	1	122	NA	414
Tenure				
< 1	18	226	223	176
1-5	217	1028	861	812
6-10	93	1139	658	899
11-15	69	620	443	497
> 15	237	1383	982	1196
Race				
White	NA	4170	NA	3339
Black	NA	123	NA	137
Spanish surname	NA	54	NA	14
Other or no answer	NA	23	NA	32

[a]Totals may not equal sample size due to omitted responses. The specific sample characteristics for Sample I are not available.
[b]Not available.

lion workers of this very decentralized organization in an attempt to maximize generalizability. The total sample size (n = 12,971) represents approximately 5 percent of the employee population of the Sears organization. Table 1 presents a summary of the sample characteristics.

A brief description of each sample follows:

I. N = 1,000—a random sample from responses made by 120,000 full-time retail employees stratified by position (retail sales, retail supervisory, and sales support) from all parts of the United States. Data collected from 1972-74.

II. N = 653—half first level supervisors from catalog order divisions and six different states; half retail sales employees from East, Midwest, South, Southwest, and Pacific Coast Territories. Stratified by sex. Data collected in 1975.

III. N = 4,421—a 25 percent random cluster sample of exempt personnel from field support units. From East, Midwest, South, Southwest, Pacific Coast, and International territories. Data collected in 1974.

IV. N = 3,287—a sample composed of all exempt corporate personnel from the Chicago and New York corporate offices. Data collected in 1971.

V. N = 3,610—a sample composed of all exempt corporate personnel from the Chicago and New York corporate offices. Data collected in 1974.

. . . .

Procedures • The forty-two items from all eight IOR scales were administered to samples I and II. Six of the IOR scales (physical conditions of work and co-workers scales were omitted for organizational reasons) were administered to samples III, IV, and V. All administrations were conducted by employees of the participating organization, on company time.

Analyses • . . . Factor analyses . . . were conducted on the IOR items for each sample. . . . This procedure allows a comparison of the resultant structure to the *a priori* structure of the

TABLE 2   Eight-Factor Rotation of 42 IOR Items—Sample I (n = 1,000).

A Priori Scale		Factor							
		I	II	III	IV	V	VI	VII	VIII
Supervision	1	68	13	−18	13	18	10	−16	−17
	2	−54	−18	17	−15	−19	−12	15	15
	3	−64	−15	14	−12	−18	−13	20	13
	4	60	13	−15	07	11	14	−01	−12
	5	63	−15	14	−14	−16	−14	15	03
	6	55	16	−16	13	07	10	−09	−12
Kind of work	1	27	57	−10	12	21	14	−13	−08
	2	10	−51	12	−13	−17	−22	15	20
	3	−17	−58	16	−14	−18	−18	13	15
	4	−07	−65	17	−10	−20	−16	09	12
	5	18	76	−16	10	15	15	−14	−05
	6	24	69	−16	12	13	11	−08	−04
Amount of work	1	11	00	−19	13	08	02	−57	−06
	2	17	−22	19	−12	−17	−15	54	08
	3	22	24	−19	13	19	15	−61	−09
	4	15	−20	18	−15	−13	−15	67	14
Financial	1	14	12	−17	71	12	08	−19	−13
	2	−11	−12	15	−57	−14	−14	04	21
	3	−09	−08	12	−66	−11	−02	04	10
	4	27	14	−20	50	24	09	−18	−02
	5	21	20	−13	56	21	10	−22	−01
Career future	1	−19	−25	13	−19	−63	−08	13	24
	2	29	20	−15	22	60	13	−14	−10
	3	22	20	−16	24	55	14	−20	−11
	4	23	24	−16	22	50	10	−10	−07
	5	−10	−19	05	−08	−44	−10	11	11
Company identifica-tion	1	34	34	−14	19	29	13	−15	−38
	2	33	−22	19	−24	−22	−13	20	57
	3	18	−29	13	−10	−21	−16	12	36
	4	34	28	−17	23	21	06	−07	−50
	5	−25	−09	13	−21	−17	−07	15	43
Co-workers	1	10	13	−10	−06	05	66	−03	−06
	2	14	17	15	05	12	70	−10	−03
	3	−17	−19	12	−10	−14	−60	19	04
	4	−21	−20	17	−11	−08	−51	08	12
	5	−33	−13	18	−20	−17	−22	19	11
Physical conditions	1	30	27	−42	10	04	15	−01	−15
	2	14	12	−78	13	12	09	−14	−11
	3	−13	−15	67	−14	−14	−12	17	06
	4	−16	−15	63	−16	−11	−13	13	12
	5	−20	−16	71	−16	−09	−10	18	08
	6	21	13	−67	15	09	18	−21	−03
Unrotated eigenvalues		14.0	1.75	1.57	1.28	1.05	.97	.70	.59

scales. In addition, the factorial solutions may be compared across samples. . . .

Results

. . . Sample I produced a solution which reproduced the eight *a priori* scales with only one stray loading (one co-worker item appeared to be measuring satisfaction with both co-workers and supervision). In sample II, the *a priori* company identification items loaded on a single factor with the *a priori* career future items (it was not possible to distinguish between company identification and career future satisfaction). All other *a priori* scales were reproduced perfectly. . . .

Factor analyses with rotation of six factors were conducted for the thirty-one items from six scales for each of the five samples. As in the previous eight-factor solution, *a priori* company identification items loaded on a single factor with *a priori* career future items for sample II. In the other four samples, however, the six *a priori* scales were reproduced either perfectly (samples I and IV) or with only one stray loading (in samples III and V . . .). Table 3 shows a representative solution (from sample IV).

To allow direct comparisons of the six factor solutions from the five samples, factor congruency estimates (Harman, 1971) were calculated between factors defining the same *a priori* scales. . . . These clearly showed that the factorial solutions, with the exception of company identification factors, are highly stable across samples ranging from retail sales clerks through top level executives and over time (samples IV and V were parallel samples with administrations separated by a three-year period.) This means that the items appear to tap the same information over a period of time with many different types of workers.

Reliability Evidence • Table 4 presents the reliability estimates for the IOR from each of the five samples. These data show that the IOR possesses very good reliability in each of the five samples. . . . Phase I of this study has demonstrated that, with few exceptions, the IOR items reliably and consistently measure various factors as intended.

TABLE 3 Six-Factor Rotation of 21 IOR Items—Sample IV ($n = 3,287$).

A Priori Scale		Factor					
		I	II	III	IV	V	VI
Supervision	1	18	78	14	11	17	10
	2	−18	−78	−15	−09	−16	−11
	3	−16	−67	−09	−08	−14	−12
	4	11	60	07	13	13	06
	5	09	73	12	17	13	10
	6	−21	−75	−11	−13	−21	−13
Kind of work	1	80	12	04	18	11	09
	2	82	12	07	18	14	12
	3	−70	−13	−13	−10	−10	−02
	4	−61	−17	−09	−10	−13	−06
	5	66	18	04	18	18	11
	6	−70	−21	−08	−17	−18	−07
Amount of work	1	−22	−19	−14	−11	−12	−64
	2	29	18	09	14	13	62
	3	−17	−15	−11	−13	−12	−54
	4	−14	01	11	03	−00	49
Financial	1	12	13	66	19	17	13
	2	15	22	54	27	20	14
	3	−07	−09	−73	−12	−06	−08
	4	−10	−06	−61	−17	−07	−09
	5	−01	12	78	17	07	13
Career future	1	−21	−23	−19	−25	−69	−09
	2	25	23	18	28	65	11
	3	21	27	22	31	48	16
	4	17	23	14	19	49	02
	5	−15	−21	−02	−06	−37	−13
Company identification	1	−08	−11	−19	−37	−08	−11
	2	19	14	26	66	20	11
	3	−16	−10	−10	−45	−14	−05
	4	−14	−12	−32	−64	−14	−11
	5	27	16	15	62	21	08
Unrotated eigenvalues		9.62	2.23	1.95	1.07	.94	.62

TABLE 4   Reliability Values for IOR In All Five Samples.[a]

Scale/Sample	I	II	III	IV	V
Supervision	.86	.88	.90	.92	.91
Kind of work	.89	.89	.87	.91	.88
Amount of work	.84	.77	.85	.77	.68
Co-workers	.80	.75	—	—	—
Physical conditions	.90	.90	—	—	—
Financial	.85	.86	.83	.85	.87
Career future	.84	.83	.84	.83	.80
Company identification	.83	.87	.81	.82	.81

[a]Reliability estimates are based on the Kuder-Richardson method of internal consistency with Spearman-Brown corrections.

PHASE II: MULTITRAIT-MULTIMETHOD STUDY

Method

Subjects • The subjects for phase II were those from sample II. Sample II included 653 employees of Sears. This sample was stratified by: (a) sex; (b) job (first-level catalog order division supervisors/retail sales); and (c) territory.

Instruments and procedures • In addition to the eight scales from the IOR, eight male/female Faces Scales were presented to tap the same eight facets of job satisfaction. The JDI, which measures five of the eight facets (supervision, work, co-workers, pay, and promotions), was included, as was the MSQ, which taps twenty facets, six of which appeared to correspond to IOR scales (supervision-human relations, co-workers, working conditions, compensation, advancement, and company policies and practices). The four sets of scales were placed within a single questionnaire which was identified as a "University of Wisconsin Job Satisfaction Study. . . ." Questionnaires were administered on the job, on company time, by company employees.

Analyses • Four methods of measuring job satisfaction were utilized. Each of these measured some or all of the eight job satisfaction facets tapped by the IOR. These multiple methods of measuring multiple "traits" were placed into a multitrait-multimethod matrix (Campbell and Fiske, 1959) for an examination of the convergent and discriminant validities of the four sets of scales. . . .

TABLE 5   Multitrait-Multimethod Matrix[a]—Sample II ($n = 622$).

Columns are grouped by method: Method 1 (IOR) = $A_1 B_1 C_1 D_1 E_1 F_1 G_1 H_1$; Method 2 (Faces) = $A_2 B_2 C_2 D_2 E_2 F_2 G_2 H_2$; Method 3 (JDI) = $A_3 B_3 C_3 D_3 E_3 F_3 G_3 H_3$; Method 4 (MSQ) = $A_4 B_4 C_4 D_4 E_4 F_4 G_4 H_4$.

Traits		A_1	B_1	C_1	D_1	E_1	F_1	G_1	H_1	A_2	B_2	C_2	D_2	E_2	F_2	G_2	H_2	A_3	B_3	C_3	D_3	E_3	F_3	G_3	H_3	A_4	B_4	C_4	D_4	E_4	F_4	G_4	H_4
Method 1 (IOR)																																	
A_1 Supervision	(76)	(76)																															
B_1 Kind of work	(77)	52	(77)																														
C_1 Amount of work	(60)	52	52	(60)																													
D_1 Co-workers	(70)	48	47	44	(70)																												
E_1 Physical conditions	(74)	47	46	46	47	(74)																											
F_1 Financial	(74)	32	41	41	49		(74)																										
G_1 Career future	(72)	53	56	47	47	64	62	(72)																									
H_1 Company identification	(74)	56	56	48	50	65	65	77	(74)																								
Method 2 (Faces)																																	
A_2 Supervision		65	39	36	44	43	28	48	50																								
B_2 Kind of work		35	58	38	42	43	37	49	51	58																							
C_2 Amount of work		46	47	53	39	45	42	50	51	61	69																						
D_2 Co-workers		29	29	24	51	36	28	36	36	61	58	49																					
E_2 Physical conditions		30	32	31	28	55	29	36	36	49	45	53	46																				
F_2 Financial		31	36	29	32	36	64	53	52	48	52	53	43	45																			
G_2 Career future		39	43	36	38	44	44	67	57	57	57	55	52	43	66																		
H_2 Company identification		43	46	39	43	47	46	56	62	59	65	64	56	59	59	61																	
Method 3 (JDI)																																	
A_3 Supervision	(87)	44	16		24	23	14	20	23	46	20	27	22	17	17	18	18	(87)															
B_3 Work	(84)	30	51	29	32	29	28	34	36	29	41	39	26	27	26	31	30	57	(84)														
D_3 Co-workers	(88)	36	32	30	50	37	33	38	43	38	37	34	41	20	27	36	35	57	59		(88)												
E_3 Pay	(70)	12	14	14	16	07	45	19	24	10	12	23	05	24	44	18	16	31	39		29	(70)											
G_3 Promotions	(79)	27	24	18	20	23	25	39	30	26	23	29	12	28	28	35	24	38	47		38	46		(79)									
Method 4 (MSQ)																																	
A_4 Supervision—human relations	(71)	71	38	43	45	41	30	49	47	66	35	45	32	30	38	36		50	27		37	18		29		(71)							
D_4 Co-workers	(79)	41	35	36	61	34	38	42	40	42	37	39	50	31	29	36	42	25	27		46	16		23		59			(79)				
E_4 Working conditions	(75)	33	39	36	36	64	36	47	45	32	33	39	27	69	35	36	41	16	26		26	24		28		45			51	(75)			
F_4 Compensation	(76)	34	36	39	33	35	70	54	52	28	32	41	23	37	68	43	42	17	29		34	58		32		44			45	54	(76)		
G_4 Advancement	(78)	46	44	39	39	45	45	68	57	45	43	48	30	41	50	60	48	22	33		34	33		62		55			52	55	64	(78)	
H_4 Company policies and practices	(63)	56	48	46	48	51	53	65	70	51	42	48	32	37	51	50	56	28	35		39	33		39		66			57	58	66	71	(63)

[a]Validity Diagonals are underlined. Reliability values are in parentheses. Heterotrait-monomethod triangles are enclosed by solid lines. Heterotrait-heteromethod triangles are enclosed by broken lines.

Results

. . . .

        Campbell and Fiske claim that several aspects bear upon
the question of validity in a multitrait-multimethod matrix (see
Table 5). These criteria were examined for the total sample and
for each sex and job subsample. The first requirement is that
validity values (correlations of different methods of measuring
the same trait) be significantly different from zero and sufficiently large to encourage further examination of validity. For
example, the IOR and JDI questions should provide the same
information about satisfaction with pay. All methods of measuring all satisfaction facets met this criterion for the total sample
and subsamples $(p < .0001)$, thus providing evidence of convergent validity. Table 6 shows the average convergent validity values for each method. The IOR method provided the highest convergent validity coefficients for the kind of work, amount of
work, company identification, and co-workers facets. The MSQ
provided the highest convergent validity coefficients for the
physical work, compensation, career future, and supervision
facets. The JDI provided the lowest validity coefficients for the
five facets measured by that method. Overall, the MSQ provided
the highest average convergent validities, followed by the IOR,
the Faces, and the JDI. For the JDI, convergent validity values
were significantly lower for females than for males. This means
that the JDI satisfaction scores for women differed somewhat
from those scores obtained by using the other instruments. There
were no sex or job differences in convergent validity for the IOR,
MSQ, or Faces.
        Campbell and Fiske provided three discriminant validity
criteria to determine whether it is possible to separate the various aspects of satisfaction. The first of these criteria requires that

TABLE 6   Convergent Validities of Methods Averaged Across Job
            Satisfaction Facets.

Method	Total Sample	Male	Female	Supervisory	Retail
IOR	59	63	57	60	61
Faces	56	61	53	56	59
JDI	47	55	43	53	48
MSQ	63	66	60	63	63

the convergent validity value for a variable should be higher than the correlations obtained between that variable and any other variable having neither trait nor method in common. Each method of measuring each satisfaction facet met this criterion in at least 98 percent of all cases for the total sample and for each subsample.

The second discriminant validity criterion requires that the convergent validity of each trait exceed the correlations between that trait and other traits measured with the same method. For example, IOR pay satisfaction should be more highly correlated with MSQ pay satisfaction than with IOR supervision satisfaction. This more stringent criterion requires that common trait variance exceed common method variance. That is, the scores appear to be influenced more by the underlying satisfaction facet than simply by the method of measurement. As Table 7 shows, this test of discriminant validity is met in 77 percent of the cases for the IOR method, 70 percent of the MSQ cases, and 55 percent of the cases for both the Faces and the JDI. While all of these proportions are statistically significant (p < .01), it should be noted that Campbell and Fiske had intended that these values approach 1.0. The proportion of .77 for the IOR method is certainly good, while the proportion of .55 for the JDI and Faces is perhaps marginal. These values were significantly lower for females than for males with all four methods. Similarly, these values were significantly lower for retail employees than for supervisory employees with all but the MSQ method. This means that the facets were not differentiated as well by the female and retail employees. For example, satisfaction with pay and promotion were confounded somewhat more by these groups than by males, particularly male supervisors.

TABLE 7 Proportion of Convergent Validity Exceeding Hetero-Mono Values (Discriminant Validity Criterion 2).[a]

Method	Total	Male	Female	P	Supervisory	Retail	P
IOR	77	86	73	.01	90	77	.004
Faces	55	74	61	.02	69	52	.005
JDI	55	75	43	.001	79	52	.003
MSQ	70	80	65	.03	74	74	n.s.

[a]Cell values indicate proportion of cases meeting the criterion for each method. P < .01 for all cases.

The final discriminant validity criterion states that the pattern of trait intercorrelations should be replicated within all heterotrait-monomethod and heterotrait-heteromethod triangles. That is, the facet scores should have similar relationships to each other regardless of the method used. This pattern is somewhat difficult to assess given the size of the triangles and the missing data. It would appear, however, that this criterion is also, at least marginally, met in the present data. To assess this criterion for the four facets common to the four methods, Kendall's coefficient of concordance was calculated by rank-ordering the correlation coefficients in each triangle (Siegel, 1956). The MSQ has high values across each subsample. The JDI, however, has low values (.41 for total sample) for this criterion relative to the other methods. The IOR and Faces values are high in the combined sample (.61 and .56) but somewhat inconsistent across subsamples—particularly for the sex comparison. With the exception of the JDI value for the male sample, which is significant at the .05 level, all other values are significant at the .01 level. Overall, this criterion (for discriminant validity) appears to be best met with males and supervisory personnel samples.

The results of the multitrait-multimethod matrix analysis have shown that all methods of measuring the various satisfaction facets possess some degree of both convergent and discriminant validity. The rank-order in which the four methods demonstrated convergent validity was: MSQ, IOR, Faces, and JDI. The rank-order in which the methods demonstrated discriminant validity was: IOR, MSQ, Faces, and JDI. It should also be noted from Table 3 that reliability estimates for the various scales show that, overall, the JDI has the highest reliability, followed by the MSQ, and then the IOR. (Reliability was good for each of these measures.) Reliability was not assessed for the Faces Scales.

DISCUSSION AND CONCLUSIONS

The analyses reported in this paper demonstrate that the IOR scales adequately meet the criteria set forth by Smith et al. (1969) for good measures of job satisfaction. The factor analyses have shown that the various facets of satisfaction can be clearly distinguished from one another and that the several items used for each facet appear to measure the same constructs. Further evidence of this discriminant validity is obtained from the various comparisons made within the Campbell and Fiske multitrait-multimethod matrix. The second Smith et al. criterion was for convergent validity. The multitrait-multimethod analysis demonstrated that the IOR measures of eight satisfaction facets agreed with three other methods of measurement. The IOR scales were shown to produce virtually identical factorial structure across five different samples of workers and across time, reflecting upon the flexibility of the instrument for use with a wide range of persons from a wide range of jobs and a variety of situations. The scales have been successfully used for hundreds of thousands of measurements with little difficulty. Respondents have ranged from unskilled workers to top-level executives. Examination of the straightforward items in the IOR scales reveals that the measures are intuitively understandable, as desired by Smith et al. The last three of their requirements are also met, as the instrument is short, easy to administer or self-administer, allows group administration of large size, and requires low expenditures of time and money due to its simplicity, ease of scoring, etc. The most critical shortcoming identified was with the company identification scale, which is the most general of the eight scales and which produces the lowest discriminant validity. This scale may be a somewhat complex measure and should be used with caution.

The multitrait-multimethod analyses of the total sample also provided evidence of the convergent and discriminant validity of the other three methods of job satisfaction measurement. Overall, the MSQ provided the highest convergent validity, although the IOR scales were best for four of the eight job satisfaction facets. The JDI provided the lowest convergent validity estimates. All methods met the Campbell and Fiske basic discriminant validity criterion. The most stringent discriminant validity criterion was met best by the IOR method and least well by the JDI and Faces.

The findings from the analyses of the sex and job subsample demonstrated that validity evidence may be sample specific. The JDI had convergent validity differences when the sample was divided by sex. In addition, all four methods of measuring job satisfaction had some problems with discriminant validity when samples were divided into sex or job groupings. The MSQ was least affected by sex and job differences followed by the IOR. The JDI was most affected by both sex and job differences. Validity differences as a function of sex and job could lead to artifactual findings for various types of samples and for tests of hypotheses involving sex or job type as either dependent or independent variables. The selection of instruments should be made carefully in light of the current findings.

In summary, it appears that the IOR method provides a means of measuring multiple facets of job satisfaction which is useful across many types of subjects and jobs over time. This method is simple, inexpensive, requires a minimum of language skills, and compares very favorably with other methods of measuring job satisfaction.

REFERENCES

Campbell, D. T. and Fiske, D. W. Convergent and discriminant validation by the multitrait-multimethod matrix. *Psychological Bulletin,* 1959, 56:81–105.

Dunham, R. B. and Herman, J. B. Development of a female faces scale for measuring job satisfaction. *Journal of Applied Psychology,* 1975, 60:629–31.

Harman, H. H. *Modern Factor Analysis.* University of Chicago Press, 1971.

Kunin, T. The construction of a new type of attitude measure. *Personnel Psychology,* 1955, 8:65–78.

Siegel, S. *Nonparametric Statistics.* McGraw-Hill, 1975.

Smith, F. J. The index of organizational reactions. *JSAS Catalog of Selected Documents in Psychology,* 1976, 6:Ms. No. 1265.

Smith, F. J. Problems and trends in the operational use of employee attitude measurements. Paper presented at the annual meeting of the American Psychological Association, 1962.

Smith, P. C. Some applications of industrial psychology to general problems of human motivation. *Proceedings of the 15th International Congress of Psychology,* 1957, 354–56.

Smith, P. C., Kendall, L. M., and Hulin, C. L. *The Measurement of Satisfaction in Work and Retirement.* Rand McNally, 1969.

Weiss, D. J., Dawis, R. V., England, G. W., and Lofquist, L. H. *Manual for the Minnesota Satisfaction Questionnaire,* Minnesota Studies in Vocational Rehabilitation: XXII. University of Minnesota Industrial Relations Center, Work Adjustment Project, 1967.

Index